Advance praise for

The EQ Interview

"Adele Lynn's newest book, destined to be a bestseller, captures the vital importance and necessity of behavioral interviewing for emotional intelligence. I find myself not being able to put this book down!"

—John Dickson, President and CEO, Redstone SeniorCare

"Selecting the right candidate is critical. Without question, *The EQ Interview* will enable me to make far more intelligent and informed hiring decisions."

—Bill Abbate, Director, Excell Technologies

"The great challenge of recruiters is how to identify emotional intelligence in potential candidates. *The EQ Interview* gives us a practical guide and excellent tool to identify professionals with these skills."

—Lúcia Helena M. Meili, Human Resources Director,
MPD Engenharia, São Paulo, Brazil

"Using the tools in *The EQ Interview,* recruiters and hiring managers will get a more complete view of a candidate's qualifications, which is sure to result in better hiring decisions."

—Jane Patterson, President, Begin Again Group, Inc.

"When the concepts outlined in this book are done correctly, the hiring manager and/or recruiter can directly influence the overall morale, teaming, interpersonal as well as organizational effectiveness and productivity of the organization."

—Franky Johnson, Johnson & Lee Consulting, LLC

The EQ Interview

Finding Employees
with High Emotional Intelligence

Adele B. Lynn

American Management Association

New York • Atlanta • Brussels • Chicago • Mexico City • San Francisco
Shanghai • Tokyo • Toronto • Washington, D.C.

This publication is designed to provide accurate and authoritative information in regard to the subject matter covered. It is sold with the understanding that the publisher is not engaged in rendering legal, accounting, or other professional service. If legal advice or other expert assistance is required, the services of a competent professional person should be sought.

Library of Congress Cataloging-in-Publication Data

Lynn, Adele B.
    The EQ interview : finding employees with high emotional intelligence / Adele B. Lynn.
        p. cm.
    Includes index.
    ISBN 978-0-8144-0941-1
    1. Employee selection.   2. Emotional intelligence—Examinations, questions, etc.   3. Core competencies.   4. Employment interviewing.
    5. Work—Psychological aspects.   I. Title.   II. Title: Employees with high emotional intelligence.

HF5549.5.S38L96 2008
658.3'1125—dc22
                                                                2008001437

The Society for Human Resource Management (SHRM) is the world's largest professional association devoted to human resource management. Our mission is to serve the needs of HR professionals by providing the most current and comprehensive resources, and to advance the profession by promoting HR's essential, strategic role. Founded in 1948, SHRM represents more than 230,000 individual members in over 125 countries, and has a network of more than 575 affiliated chapters in the United States, as well as offices in China and India. Visit SHRM at www.shrm.org.

PRINTING NUMBER

10 9 8 7 6 5 4

CONTENTS

1 Introduction   1

**2 The Five Areas of Emotional Intelligence
and the EQ Job Competencies**   7

3 Self-Awareness   15

Competency 1: Impact on Others   16

Competency 2: Emotional and Inner Awareness   20

*Competency 3: Accurate Assessment of Skills
and Abilities*   26

4 Self-Control or Self-Management   33

Competency 1: Emotional Expression   35

Competency 2: Courage or Assertiveness   39

Competency 3: Resilience   42

Competency 4: Planning the Tone of Conversations   47

5 Empathy   53

Competency 1: Respectful Listening   54

Competency 2: Feeling the Impact on Others   56

Competency 3: Service Orientation   58

6 Social Expertness   65

Competency 1: Building Relationships   68

Competency 2: Collaboration   71

Competency 3: Conflict Resolution   74

Competency 4: Organizational Savvy   78

123228

7 Personal Influence: Influencing Self   85

Competency 1: Self-Confidence   86

Competency 2: Initiative and Accountability   91

Competency 3: Goal Orientation   94

Competency 4: Optimism   98

Competency 5: Flexibility and Adaptability   101

8 Personal Influence: Influencing Others   111

Competency 1: Leading Others   112

Competency 2: Creating a Positive Work Climate   116

Competency 3: Getting Results Through Others   121

9 Mastery of Purpose and Vision   129

Competency 1: Understanding One's Purpose and Values   130

Competency 2: Taking Actions Toward One's Purpose   133

Competency 3: Authenticity   135

10 The EQ Fraud and Other Warning Signs   141

All One-Sided: Too Good to Be True   142

Other Behavior Trends   146

A Word About Instinct   151

11 A Final Word   153

**Appendix 1. Emotional Intelligence Table
of Competencies**   157

Appendix 2. Questions by Area and Competencies   161

Index   181

About the Author   185

CHAPTER 1

Introduction

Fundamental emotional intelligence (EQ) competencies lie beneath great performance for nearly every job tackled by today's workforce. For a hiring manager or interviewer, including these competencies as part of the interview process begs consideration. We're not suggesting that technical skills and abilities be taken for granted. Skills and technical competence must always serve a prominent role in the assessment process. However, a growing body of evidence points to the fact that when technical competencies are equal, EQ competencies account for job success in many different positions. In fact, for some positions, EQ competencies account for a larger portion of job success than technical competencies. Leadership IQ, a training and research center that teaches executive and management best practices, conducted a study of more than twenty thousand employees that tracked the success and failure of new hires. After interviewing 5,247 managers, the study's researchers concluded that only 11 percent of employees failed because they lacked the technical competence to do the job. The remaining reasons new hires failed were issues such as alienating coworkers, being unable to accept feedback, lack of ability to manage emotions, lack of motivation or drive, and poor interpersonal skills.[1] These results provide a good indication that including comprehensive EQ competencies as part of the interview process gives hiring managers and interviewers access to new and critical information to predict a candidate's effectiveness.

As baby boomers become eligible for retirement and begin to exit the workforce, employers grapple with how to hire and train enough workers to fill the void. According to the Bureau of Labor Statistics, 20 percent of the workforce will be over age fifty-five by 2010. In 2004, the number of people age forty and older in the workforce is over 56 percent.[2] Companies face large numbers of new hires who will view the organization much differently than do the employees who are leaving. Commitment and retention will be a challenge because these new hires will have little invested in a company. As a result, they will have little incentive to stay for the long term if they receive a more lucrative offer from another firm. If the hiring company doesn't meet the new hire's expectations, that new hire will leave—causing an endless hiring-resignation cycle and a resultant gap in the skills and abilities needed for the company to compete. And this cycle will prove costly. Turnover costs range from 120 to 200 percent of annual salary, and new employee performance takes thirteen months to reach maximum efficiency. These statistics offer another compelling reason to screen for emotional intelligence competencies. Organizational commitment and retention are closely linked to emotional intelligence.[3] Few would argue that commitment and retention are not useful traits. Retention links directly to job satisfaction. Job satisfaction is related to self-esteem, emotional stability, and conscientiousness.[4] The emotional intelligence model in this book takes all of these elements into consideration.

To address and plan for future manpower needs, organizations perform skills audits that take into account the technical skills that will be needed once the baby boomers exit. Granted, hiring and training people for technical skills begins to fill the technical void or brain drain, but since various studies estimate that emotional intelligence competencies account for anywhere from 24 to 69 percent of performance success, companies waste their recruitment efforts if they don't consider screening methods aimed at a candidate's emotional intelligence.[5] In addition to auditing the technical gap, companies must begin to audit and map the skills and competencies beyond technical excellence that drive the organization's success. What defines a company's outstanding service orientation? What makes a company nimble enough to act on market-driven changes? What inspires the innovation and creativity that keep a company competitive? What forces drive the integrity of and trust in a brand? These are not technical competencies by nature. Although technical excellence is a competitive factor that can't be ignored, the competencies that drive these intangible market advantages are propelled by the very core, or fundamental, competencies that define *how* a company does things.

The organization's objective becomes hiring people who can deliver the *how* consistent with the company's success. The interview process gives the hiring manager and interviewer a unique opportunity to determine *how* people accomplish results, not just what they accomplish. This insight into how people accomplish results allows the hiring manager and interviewer to assess whether or not the person will fit within the organization. They can assess whether the potential new hire will contribute in a way that aligns with the organization's values and behave in a way that is consistent with the company's competitive advantage—or whether the candidate's behavior will collide with the organization's goals. Poor fit is one of the three most likely causes of employee turnover.[6] Research suggests that fit, not skill or education, is the most common reason people fail. Fit also plays a significant role in turnover due to job dissatisfaction.

This book assists hiring managers and interviewers to assess EQ competencies. It gives hiring managers and interviewers a description of each of the EQ competencies, examples of the EQ competencies in the workplace in various types of jobs, interview questions for each of the EQ competencies, and analyses of responses to the suggested questions. With these tools, hiring managers and interviewers can evaluate and construct an interview plan that gives them a more complete picture of the candidates' abilities to succeed.

Not all jobs require all the EQ competencies covered in this book. However, because emotional intelligence is so fundamental to our ability to interact with people, many jobs require at least some of these competencies. The hiring manager and interviewer must decide which competencies contribute to success in the position they are hiring for. Then the hiring manager or interviewer should select interview questions that represent these competencies. Some of the questions in this book are aimed at managers or leaders; however, most are acceptable for all job levels. We encourage the interviewer and hiring manager to record the questions asked as well as the responses. If multiple candidates are to be interviewed, a consistent approach and consistent questions produce the most unbiased results.

Behavior-based interviewing forms the fundamental theoretical base for the questions in this book. Behavior-based interviewing examines past behavior and how that behavior contributes to a person's success. Behavior-based interviewing in a structured format has the highest validity of all interviewing tools, according to a study by Ryan and Tippins from Michigan State University.[7] Unfortunately, some managers rely solely on the tools of gut instinct and chemistry to predict a person's effectiveness. We recommend behavior-based interviewing, following a defined structure, and noting and rating answers based on a Likert scale as the most useful methods for interviewing candidates. We believe that these methods give the interviewer important data to quantify gut instincts and overall impressions.

To gain an understanding of emotional intelligence, the interviewer will examine the very nature of the behaviors that led to successful results. We believe it is possible for a candidate to have very successful results while at the same time wreaking havoc on peers or others within the organization. The questions in this book examine the behavioral consequences or impact of the successful results, not just the results. For example, a line manager may have a great production record in his unit, but may have accomplished this goal by ignoring the needs of peers and may in fact be blind to the goals of the organization. Alternatively, long-term goals and results may be sacrificed for short-term numbers.

It is also possible for certain behaviors to create a successful outcome, yet not take into consideration the motives or intentions of the candidate. Therefore, on many of the questions, the effective interviewer or hiring manager will listen for the thought patterns that preceded and those that followed a particular behavior. This gives the interviewer insights into the intentions behind the behavior as expressed by the candidate. The interviewer won't be in the position of making judgments about the candidate's intentions, but instead will be directed to listen to the facts about the candidate's intentions as reported in reflection by the candidate herself.

Candidates will also be directed to reflect on times when their outcomes or results didn't meet their intentions. By asking candidates to reflect on their results, interviewers encourage candidates to reveal behavior patterns that can dramatically affect teamwork, service orientation, helpfulness, respectfulness, persistence, reaction to failure, resilience, and other important EQ competencies. This helps the interviewer and hiring manager understand how candidates use past experiences and integrate them into their current behavior.

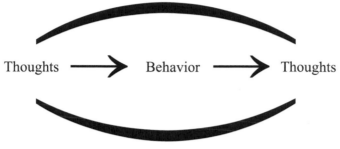

Thoughts Precede and Follow Behavior

Endnotes

1. "Leadership IQ Study: Why New Hires Fail," *PR Newswire,* September 20, 2005, 1.
2. Ellen Galinsky, "The Changing Landscape of Work," *Generations* (Spring 2007): 7.
3. Chi-Sum Wong and Kenneth S. Law, "The Effects of Leader and Follower Emotional Intelligence on Performance and Attitude: An Exploratory Study," *Leadership Quarterly* (June 2002): 243.
4. "Job Performance Linked to Personality," *Industrial Engineer* 39, 7 (July 2007): 11.
5. V.U. Druskat, F. Sala, and G. Mount, eds., *Linking Emotional Intelligence and Performance at Work* (Mahwah, NJ: Lawrence Erlbaum Associates, 2006).
6. Nancy Gardner, "Should I Stay or Should I Go? What Makes Employees Voluntarily Leave or Keep Their Jobs," University of Washington Office of News and Information, July 26, 2007, http://uwnews.washington .edu/ni/article.asp?articleID=31234.
7. Ann Marie Ryan and Nancy T. Tippins, "Attracting and Selecting: What Psychological Research Tells Us," *Human Resource Management* 43, 4 (Winter 2004): 305.

CHAPTER 2

The Five Areas
of Emotional Intelligence
and the EQ Job Competencies

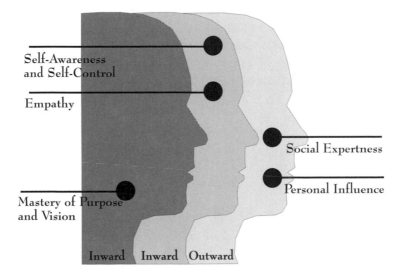

Emotional intelligence is defined as a person's ability to manage herself as well as her relationships with others so that she can live her intentions. Very often, emotional intelligence is misunderstood. In fact, many people think that emotional intelligence is equivalent to social skills. Thinking that emotional intelligence is social skills, however, is like thinking that a car is a steering wheel. This viewpoint simply misses a huge part of the picture. Social skills are about our re-lationship with the external world—how we interact with others. Of course, those skills make up a part of the EQ competencies, but so much of emotional intelligence is about our internal world. And it is our in-ternal world that will drive how we interact with and respond to the external world. Emotional intelligence, therefore, includes skills that drive our internal world, as well as our response to the external world.

Our model for emotional intelligence contains five areas: self-awareness and control, empathy for others, social expertness, personal influence, and mastery of purpose.[1] Within the five areas, several spe-cific competencies emerge. See Figure 2.1 and Appendix 1 for the Table of Competencies. Definitions and competency descriptions of the five areas are as follows:

1. *Self-awareness and self-control* comprise one's ability to fully under-stand oneself and to use that information to manage emotions productively. This area includes the competencies of accurate un-derstanding of one's emotions and the impact emotions have on performance, accurate assessment of strengths and weaknesses, understanding one's impact on others, and self-management or self-control, including managing anger, disappointment, or failure (resulting in resilience) and managing fear (resulting in courage).

2. *Empathy* is the ability to understand the perspective of others. This area includes the competencies of listening to others, under-standing others' points of view, understanding how one's words and actions affect others, and wanting to be of service to others.

3. *Social expertness* is the ability to build genuine relationships and bonds and express caring, concern, and conflict in healthy ways. This area includes the competencies of building relationships, or-ganizational savvy, collaboration, and conflict resolution.

4. *Personal influence* is the ability to positively lead and inspire oth-ers as well as oneself. This area includes the competencies of lead-ing others, creating a positive work climate, and getting results from others. It also includes self-confidence, initiative and moti-vation, optimism, and flexibility.

5. *Mastery of purpose and vision* is the ability to bring authenticity to one's life and to live out one's intentions and values. This area includes the competencies of understanding one's purpose, taking actions toward one's purpose, and being authentic.

As you can see in the model depicted in Figure 2.1, three of the components relate to our internal world (self-awareness and self-control, empathy, and mastery of purpose and vision). The other two form our relations to the external world (social expertness and personal influence). However, it is important to recognize that all are interrelated, and one component builds on the next. Without self-awareness and self-control, it is difficult, if not impossible, to improve one's relationship with the outside world. For example, if I am not aware of my actions, thoughts, and words, I have no basis for self-understanding. If I have some awareness and self-understanding, then I can ask, What is my impact on others, in my current state? If I find that impact to be negative—if I find that it detracts from my life goals —I may choose to change my actions, thoughts, or words. However, some people look at themselves, understand that their actions, words, or thoughts have a negative impact on others or detract from their life goals, yet still either choose not to change or find change too difficult to enact. In emotional intelligence, this change is what we call self-control. It is about knowing ourselves, and then deciding the appropriate volume level and expression of our emotions. How do these emotions enhance our relationships with others and our life goals, and how do they detract from them? Self-awareness and self-control are intertwined, as self-awareness alone is of little service without self-control. Leaders, teammates, and others in the workplace are interdependent, so it behooves everyone to improve self-understanding and then to act upon this knowledge.

Beyond self-awareness and self-control is empathy, which is also listed as an internal function on our model. Empathy must be felt inside before it can be reflected somehow in our relationships with people in our external world. Therefore, empathy is a turning point or transition in our emotional intelligence as it plays out in the outside world. Also, without empathy, we are incapable of comprehending the impact of our actions or words on others. We may have been told that a particular behavior or word affects others in a negative way, but empathy enables us to experience it. It also drives us to want to be helpful or of service to others.

Next in our model is social expertness. Few of us can work or live in isolation. People are generally a part of the equation. Social expertness allows us to build genuine social bonds with others. It allows us to know people in a way that is beyond knowing name, rank, and serial number. It allows us to connect with them in an honorable way. The best analogy I can offer is that it's not about the number of people in your Rolodex, but rather about the reaction those people have when you're on the other end of the phone. Are they delighted that you called, or would they rather be talking to the long-distance carrier trying to sell phone services? Beyond honorable social bonds, social expertness calls on us to invite those within our social bonds to collaborate in achieving our intentions. How well are we able to collaborate with others and blend thoughts and ideas to achieve goals or live intentions? But once we have invited people to collaborate, conflict is inevitable, as different ideas will emerge. How will we resolve those differences? Social expertness demands high levels of conflict-resolution skills, which work to preserve social bonds and trust. Social expertness also requires us to have organizational savvy in order to move ideas and goals forward while maintaining positive relationships.

Personal influence is the next area of our model for emotional intelligence. It also reflects our interactions with others. Personal influence is where true leadership emerges. Before this relationship stage, we are peer to peer; it is here that we intend to influence others toward goals or missions. However, we cannot influence others if we have not created strong bonds or invited others to collaborate, or if we lack the ability to resolve conflict in healthy ways. Leadership is not reserved for positional leaders, however; all people are leaders. Even if we think about leadership in terms of influencing our children, this area of emotional intelligence is essential for a rich life and calls on us to influence others. Equally important is our ability to influence ourselves. It is within the walls of our own souls that the most work must be done. As we influence ourselves to change, we can be an instrument of influence to others. Influencing ourselves requires our ability to take initiative, stay motivated, display confidence and optimism, and be flexible.

Finally, the model includes mastery of purpose and vision. It is the most internally seated of all the aspects of emotional intelligence, and it serves as a foundation on which to build a more emotionally intelligent life. It is, in essence, both the reason we strive for emotional intelligence and the foundation that keeps us anchored. If we know what our purpose is, it is much easier to determine what types of emotional reactions will serve our purpose and what types will defeat it. Therefore, understanding and managing emotions helps us to live our life purpose. We place it last because it is sometimes the most difficult to know and conceptualize. Although it is certainly possible to excel in all other areas of emotional intelligence without yet discovering true purpose, once true purpose is discovered, emotional intelligence will be easier to improve.

FIGURE 2.1 **Emotional Intelligence Table of Competencies**		
AREA OF EMOTIONAL INTELLIGENCE	**DEFINITION**	**COMPETENCIES**
Self-Awareness and Self-Control	The ability to fully understand oneself and one's impact on others and to use that information to manage oneself productively	*Self-Awareness* • Impact on others: An accurate understanding of how one's behavior or words affect others • Emotional and inner awareness: An accurate understanding of how one's emotions and thoughts affect behaviors • Accurate self-assessment: An honest assessment of strengths and weaknesses

(continued)

FIGURE 2.1 *Continued*

AREA OF EMOTIONAL INTELLIGENCE	DEFINITION	COMPETENCIES
		Self-Control • Emotional expression: The ability to manage anger, stress, excitement, and frustration • Courage: The ability to manage fear • Resilience: The ability to manage disappointment or failure
Empathy	Ability to understand the perspective of others	• Respectful listening: Listening respectfully to others to develop a deep understanding of others' points of view • Feeling impact on others: The ability to assess and determine how situations as well as one's words and actions affect others • Service orientation: The desire to help others
Social Expertness	Ability to build genuine relationships and bonds and express caring, concern, and conflict in healthy ways	• Building relationships: The ability to build social bonds • Collaboration: The ability to invite

FIGURE 2.1 *Continued*

AREA OF EMOTIONAL INTELLIGENCE	DEFINITION	COMPETENCIES
		others in and value their thoughts related to ideas, projects, and work • Conflict resolution: The ability to resolve differences • Organizational savvy: The ability to understand and maneuver within organizations
Personal Influence	Ability to positively lead and inspire others as well as oneself	*Influencing Others* • Leading others: The ability to have others follow you • Creating a positive work climate: The ability to create an inspiring culture • Getting results through others: The ability to achieve goals through others *Influencing Self* • Self-confidence: An appropriate belief in one's skills or abilities • Initiative and accountability: Being internally guided to take steps or actions and taking responsibility for those actions

(continued)

FIGURE 2.1 *Continued*

AREA OF EMOTIONAL INTELLIGENCE	DEFINITION	COMPETENCIES
		• Goal orientation: Setting goals for one-self and living and working toward goals • Optimism: Having a tendency to look at the bright side of things and to be hopeful for the best • Flexibility: The ability to adapt and bend to the needs of others or situations as appropriate
Mastery of Purpose and Vision	Ability to bring authenticity to one's life and live out one's intentions and values	• Understanding one's purpose and values: Having a clearly defined purpose and values • Taking actions toward one's purpose: Taking actions to advance one's purpose • Authenticity: Alignment and transparency of one's motives, actions, intentions, values, and purpose

Endnote

1. Adele Lynn, *The EQ Difference* (New York: Amacom, 2005).

CHAPTER 3

Self-Awareness

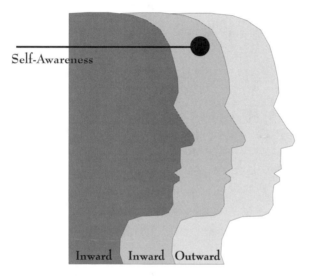

Self-Awareness

Inward   Inward   Outward

Competency 1—Impact on Others
Competency 2—Emotion and Inner Awareness
Competency 3—Accurate Assessment of Skills and Abilities

S elf-awareness is the ability to fully understand oneself and one's impact on others and to use that information to manage emotions productively. It includes three competencies:

1. *Impact on others,* which is an accurate understanding of how one's behavior or words affect others;

2. *Emotional and inner awareness,* which is an accurate understanding of how one's emotions and thoughts affect one's behaviors; and

3. *Accurate assessment of skills and abilities,* which is an accurate assessment of your strengths and weaknesses.

Understanding how one's emotions and thoughts affect one's behavior, and then understanding how one's behavior impacts one's teammates, peers, customers, vendors, and most other members of the human race, are critical and fundamental skills in emotional intelligence. When one understands the direct relationship between how one behaves and how others react, this breakthrough connection enhances one's ability to get along with others and achieve results. This revelation is at the heart of self-awareness. It is also at the center of many workplace values such as teamwork, customer service, and respect. But these values aren't just nice words that appear on the company values list. They are central to getting work done and building organizations and businesses.

Competency 1: Impact on Others

Consider the sales representative who has no idea that he just insulted a customer by directing her to a "more affordable" alternative. The customer felt insulted by the way the salesperson communicated. The sales representative said, "Well, you'd probably be better suited to our lower-price brand." The customer felt that the salesperson judged her ability to pay and felt that he was demeaning. The customer quietly left the store to find another place to spend her money. The sales representative's intentions were in fact to help the customer find the most affordable alternative. As consumers, we've all suffered these little insults. However, now research clearly links the emotional intelligence competency of self-awareness to sales performance. The research states that salespeople's performance is enhanced with emotional intelligence competencies such as self-awareness.[1]

Another painfully unaware individual, a physician, interrupted as the patient talked, thus missing an important symptom that the patient was about to reveal. In fact, statistics suggest that patients have only twelve seconds to speak before the physician interrupts.[2] Of course, the physician probably meant well. Perhaps the mounting pressures of a waiting room full of patients led to the physician's impatience.

In another example, an IT help person waltzed into an executive's office to offer tech support on a computer problem. The IT employee said nothing; instead, after a quick inspection of the problem, he shook his head and sighed. Then his fingers flew across the keyboard as he implemented a quick fix of the problem. The executive said that the tech's dismissive attitude insulted him. The tech saw this problem as a waste of his time that could have been avoided if others on his team had installed the software correctly. He wondered what he could do to avoid this problem in the future. The executive, however, read his behavior as curt and dismissive.

Yet another employee complained to the manager that a coworker routinely made comments about her in front of others that she found insulting. The coworker said she's just teasing and suggested that the employee was too thin-skinned. In fact, the coworker said she really likes the employee and thought that these little barbs kept everyone laughing and having a good time.

A common morale complaint lodged against some leaders is that they often don't say good morning. Employees criticize these leaders as lacking common courtesy and respect and setting a sour tone in the workplace. The leaders who are guilty of this infraction don't even realize that the employees feel snubbed.

All of these examples of lack of self-awareness create costs in terms of productivity and profit. In the case of health care, lack of self-awareness can also cost lives. You'll notice that the examples cut across industries, job function, and education levels. You'll notice, too, that in each of these examples, the perpetrator did not have bad intentions. In each case, the person responsible for the action was either preoccupied or even trying to be helpful. In fact, we find that most persons who behave in a manner that others find disturbing actually have good intentions. They simply are blind to how their behaviors are impacting those around them. Awareness of how our behaviors and moods affect others is a universal EQ competency that all hiring managers and interviewers should include in their interview strategy. No matter what the job, the hiring manager or interviewer should craft questions that will give some indication of a potential applicant's understanding of his impact on others.

It's also valuable for the interviewer or hiring manager to gain information with questions aimed at assessing the candidate's observation skills. Assessing whether a candidate can astutely observe herself and the impact she has on others allows the candidate to monitor her behavior. It also gives the interviewer information as to whether the candidate can read nonverbal cues and other signals and adapt her behavior accordingly. A study published in the *IT Managers Journal* found that IT professionals who had the ability to read nonverbal cues and adapt accordingly displayed better problem awareness, solution generation, and decision making.[3] A study of certified public accountants found that those who were able to read and respond to nonverbal cues were able to build more trusting relationships and to attract high-net-worth clients.[4]

Questions to Assess Impact on Others

Q: Tell me about a time when you did or said something and it had a positive impact on a coworker, a customer, or an employee.

Q: Tell me about a time when you did or said something and it had a negative impact on a coworker, a customer, or an employee.

Q: Tell me about a time when you were surprised about the positive impact your behavior or words had on a coworker, a customer, or an employee. How did you learn this information?
  • What did you do when you learned this information?

Q: Tell me about a time when you were surprised about the negative impact your behavior or words had on a coworker, a customer, or an employee.

- How did you learn this information?
- What did you do when you learned this information?

Q: Describe a time when you knew you did or said something that caused a problem for a coworker, a customer, or an employee.

- How did you know it caused a problem?

Q: Can you think of a time when someone interpreted something you said or did in a negative way, even though you didn't intend for it to be negative?

- Tell me about that.

Q: How do you know if your words or behaviors have a positive impact on others?

Q: How do you know if your words or behaviors have a negative impact on others?

Questions to Assess Observation Skills

Q: Have you ever noticed that someone at work was having a bad day?

- How did you know?
- What did you do?

Q: Have you ever decided to delay presenting an idea to someone at work because the timing wasn't right?

- What did you base that decision on?
- What did you do?

Q: Have you ever noticed that you were annoying someone at work?

- What did you base that on?
- What did you do?

Q: Have you ever been in a situation where you thought you needed to adjust or modify your behavior?

- How did you know?

KEY POINTS TO CONSIDER WHEN ASSESSING ANSWERS

Most candidates should be able to come up with an example of something they did that caused concern for others. Watch for how they incorporated this awareness into future encounters. One candidate, surprised when his boss told him that he interrupted his customers, said that he didn't believe his boss and that his boss didn't know enough about him to make that statement. Without realizing it, the candidate proved his boss's point when he interrupted the interviewer as the interviewer asked a clarifying question.

Emotional intelligence requires a person to be aware of and to read cues in different situations and then adapt accordingly. This kind of adaptability to the environment ensures success. The questions listed above give you important information about a person's awareness of these types of cues. You also learn how the person adjusts his behavior according to the cues he reads. Because a person may be reluctant to admit that he may at times annoy others, the interviewer may need to introduce the question with a comment such as, "Everyone can be annoying at some time. Would you tell me about a time when you annoyed someone at work?" As the interviewer, you can help the candidate feel at ease so that you can extract the most honest answers from the interview.

Competency 2: Emotional and Inner Awareness

Self-awareness must incorporate an accurate understanding of one's emotions and the impact that one's emotions have on performance. Athletes, performers, and others talk about being "on." But the concept of being "on" applies to all of us. If we're distracted, angry, fearful, depressed, or preoccupied, it can affect performance. It can also affect our relationships with others, including coworkers, peers, and customers at work. So self-awareness includes an awareness of our emotions and moods and an understanding of how those impact our performance. For example, the customer service representative who feels insulted by the customer on the telephone may respond differently to that customer than to a customer she considers to be pleasant and mild tempered. Yet, the customer service representative's job remains the same—to resolve the problem or situation. The customer service worker's feelings may define her behavior or performance in these interactions. Likewise, if a team member feels that her ideas are less useful than the ideas of her teammates, these feelings of self-doubt may cause her to be silent with her opinions. These feelings of self-doubt drive her behavior or performance. A basic understanding of emotions and how they affect performance forms a strong foundation of self-awareness. Because emotions often surface in our internal self-talk, awareness of our internal self-talk helps bolster self-awareness. Self-defeating self-talk may cause us to experience strong self-defeating emotions such as resentment, hostility, anxiety, depression, and the like.[5] These emotions can affect relationships and performance at work, especially if they are not acknowledged and resolved. During the interview process, the interviewer should ask questions to establish the candidate's awareness that emotions may interfere with desired behavior or results.

Triggers influence emotional reactions. Everyone has triggers. For some, walking into a messy workplace causes an instant flash of anger. For others, feeling ignored by a coworker produces an emotional reaction. People who exhibit strong self-awareness understand these triggers and the state of mind, situations, and other factors that are apt to foreshadow certain negative behaviors. When a person understands himself, he is better able to exercise restraint or control in his reactions. Interviewers and hiring managers who include questions on triggers gain insight into a candidate's self-knowledge that proves useful in interactions with customers or coworkers.

How we reflect on our past behavior also conveys important data. For example, if someone criticizes our behavior, how do we reflect on this criticism? Do we defend our actions? Do we put down the source? Or do we take the criticism and determine its usefulness? If we take the comment in and evaluate its usefulness, this can lead to improved self-awareness.[6] However, common errors often creep into our reflections. These common errors stop us from examining our own behavior. If we defend our behavior, blame others, justify, or rationalize, then it's doubtful that we'll be able to use these past experiences to change or grow. In a study of the impact of behavior that others found offensive, individuals who perpetrated the behavior had certain thought patterns as they were asked to reflect on their actions. Those thought patterns included (1) denying responsibility and instead blaming the situation on circumstances, (2) denying the significance of the action by minimizing the impact on the other person, (3) stating that the victim brought on the action by some sort of behavior on the victim's part, and (4) stating that they (the perpetrators) are not alone and that many others have engaged in the sort of behavior that they engaged in. On the contrary, when these same individuals were the victims of similar behaviors, they had a much higher sense of injustice than when they were the perpetrators of such behaviors.[7] These common reflection errors do little to mitigate the recurrence of negative behavior. However, if we reflect on our experiences and ask ourselves how we could have avoided or improved the situation, then the chances of changing behavior increase. It's important to assess how a candidate uses reflection about past experiences. Introspection and mindfulness produce positive clinical results in changing behavior and have important implications for emotional intelligence.[8] In addition, self-reflection is the key to self-fulfillment. Nothing is more valuable than deepening your sense of who you are.[9] In fact, just about all of the questions in this book will help you to understand how candidates use reflection and whether or not their reflection is riddled with the common errors listed above.

Questions to Assess Awareness of Emotions or Thoughts

Q: Tell me about a time when you were distracted or preoccupied about something.
- How did you know?
- What impact did that have on your performance?
- What impact did it have on others at work?

Q: Tell me about a time when you were in a good mood at work.
- How did that affect your performance?
- What impact did your mood have on others at work?

Q: Describe a time when you were angry about something at work.
- How did that affect your performance?
- What impact did it have on others at work?

Q: Tell me about a time when the mood or attitude of your coworkers, employees, or others affected you.

Q: Describe a time when you were aware that your mood was affecting how you were behaving at work.

Questions to Assess Awareness of Triggers

Q: Tell me about some situations or people that annoy you in your present (or previous) position.
- Tell me what you do about these situations or people.

Q: Tell me about a time when you were able to avoid a negative situation at work.
- How did you know it was going to be negative?
- Tell me what you did.

Q: Describe some situations or circumstances that bring out your best at work.
- How do you behave during those times?

Q: Describe some situations or circumstances that bring out your worst at work.
- How do you behave during those times?
- What do you do about those times?

Q: Tell me about a time when you purposely prepared yourself to deal with a situation that you knew would be negative.
- What did you do? How did it work out?

Questions to Assess Reflection Skills

Q: Tell me about a time when something that you had responsibility for at work didn't go well.

Who's fault was it? (This is a leading question—it's assuming blame. The candidate should consider his or her own role in the problem.)

Q: Tell me about a time at work when others didn't cooperate with you.

 • How would you analyze that situation?

Q: Tell me about a conflict you had at work.

 • How would you analyze that conflict?

Q: Have you ever unintentionally insulted or offended someone at work?

 • How did you handle that?

Q: Tell me about a time when you reacted to something or someone in the workplace in a way that was not aligned with your intentions.

 • What did you do after this situation?

KEY POINTS TO CONSIDER WHEN ASSESSING ANSWERS
Awareness of Emotions or Thoughts

The key information extracted by these questions indicates the candidate's awareness that emotions exist and affect self and others. Once a candidate establishes her awareness of the impact of emotions, she improves her chances of being able to manage them. Some candidates deny that feelings or emotions exist. And although it may be true that some people are much more affable than others, it's likely that at times, emotions affect all of us. With these types of questions, you can expect the interviewee to minimize the impact of the emotions, or discuss constructive actions that she takes to manage her reactions. But the bottom line is that a candidate who expresses awareness of her emotions is more likely to be able to manage her emotions than one who is unaware. Also, research demonstrates that people who are self-aware or mindful of their actions have more positive outcomes.[10] When mindful or self-aware, we are provided with a window to examine our behaviors. If a candidate flatly denies any emotions at work, the candidate may be missing an opportunity to examine her behavior.

Awareness of Triggers

The candidate who knows himself can predict or understand his triggers. In fact, understanding and predicting one's emotional reactions to situations is central to self-awareness.[11] By understanding what could cause or trigger a negative reaction, the candidate is much more likely to be able to manage himself by avoiding the situation or planning in advance for it. Look for follow-up statements that indicate that the candidate manages his reactions or takes steps to prevent the situation. When one candidate described a time when he purposely prepared himself to deal with a negative situation, he described a situation with a negative coworker. He said he knew that his coworker's negativity affected his viewpoint, so he purposely changed his lunch routine. He said he didn't find it useful to sit through lunch to hear his coworker's negative comments about the job.

These questions also give you important information about a candidate's tolerance level. In work situations, candidates must interact with many different situations and people. Therefore, learning about a person's tolerance and triggers provides useful information. You can also extract information relevant to fit. If a person relates that people and jobs that require a high level of interaction trigger a negative reaction, then it's obvious that a job requiring lots of interaction isn't an ideal fit for this candidate.

Reflection Skills

In the questions to assess reflection skills, the interviewer assesses how a person thinks or reflects about past situations. To help the candidate give straightforward answers, put the candidate at ease. Also, you may need to redirect the answer a few times because the candidate may want to focus on what she did to resolve the conflict or to get others to cooperate. Although that is important information that you should consider, the gist of the analysis should be about what the person thought about the experience. Did she rationalize? Did she assign blame to someone else? Or maybe she defended her actions as right. It's also possible that the candidate thought she was helpless. In the analysis or reflection, the person's answer should suggest that the candidate considered her own actions and what she could have done differently to be part of the solution. Holding oneself accountable would sound something like this: "Well, as I think back on this situation, I think I could have done [or said]. . . . If I had done this, I think I would have gained her cooperation sooner." This person's analysis of the situation and her behavior helps her to consider a better outcome. This positive reflection can lead to learning. However, listen for that fine line between holding oneself accountable and beating oneself up. Beating oneself up or becoming so discouraged by a situation that the person vows never to try it again may demonstrate a lack of resilience. The bottom line is that holding ourselves accountable for the results of our behavior is important and can lead to new learning. Also, holding ourselves accountable for situations such as these generally translates into holding ourselves accountable for work goals and production numbers.

Competency 3: Accurate Assessment of Skills and Abilities

Accurate assessment of skills and abilities enables reflection, appraisal, and lifelong learning.[12] When a person is blind to his skills and abilities, he is less apt to utilize them. These unrealized strengths may not be developed to their full potential. On the contrary, if a person is blind to his weaknesses or believes his skills are greater than they are, he is less open to development or feedback. This self-deception proves destructive and has performance consequences. A study in the *British Dental Journal* indicated that dental surgeons' poor performance related to removal of a third molar was due to self-deception and the desire to convey a favorable impression.[13] An article in *Training and Development* states, "When we have an inflated view of our achievements and capabilities, we are easily seduced by the approval and applause of others and we're going to make mistakes assessing our own work and take on more than we can handle."[14] Another compelling reason to search for people with accurate self-assessment comes from the *Journal of Applied Psychology,* which states that there is a positive relationship between accurate self-assessment and commitment to change.[15] Accurate self-assessment also helps people optimize the capabilities they possess and be aware of those they do not.[16] During the interview process, questions designed to correct for self-deception and inaccurate assessment of skills and abilities prove valuable.

Consider the following example. Colleen's manager spoke to her several times about her need to develop better customer service skills. Colleen believed that her boss catered too much to customer demands. She believed that her skills were fine. When asked in an interview about performance feedback she had received, Colleen said, "My manager told me that I should give in more to customer demands, but I think he should stop caving in every time a customer wants something."

Questions to Assess Accurate Assessment of Skills and Abilities

Q: Describe a time when you received feedback about your performance and were in agreement.
- What did you agree with?

Q: Describe a time when you received feedback about your performance and you disagreed with that feedback.
- What did you disagree with?

Q: Was there ever a time when you initially disagreed with feedback you received and later came to accept it?
- Tell me about that.

Q: Were you ever surprised by criticism you received?
- What was the criticism and why were you surprised?

Q: What has been a consistent strength of yours?
- What evidence do you have that this is an area in which you are strong?

Q: What has been a consistent area of development for you?
- How do you know that this is an area of development for you?

Q: List three things you have learned about yourself in the last year that are relevant to the way you work.
- How did you learn this information?
- Describe a time when you used this new information.

KEY POINTS TO CONSIDER WHEN ASSESSING ANSWERS

The interview provides the interviewer or hiring manager with an opportunity to determine if the candidate possesses an accurate assessment of her skills. People who can accurately assess both their strengths and their weaknesses operate without blind spots. They maximize their strengths and find ways to improve or mitigate their weaknesses. When a candidate accurately assesses her own skills, that candidate is in a better position to determine whether she will succeed in the job for which she is interviewing. The questions above prove difficult for candidates because they may feel a need to guard against telling the interviewer about a time when they were criticized. The interviewer must set the tone so that the candidate feels comfortable. Be sure to include questions that ask the candidate to point to evidence; the evidence helps you to determine whether the candidate bases her answers on objective data. For example, Jerry stated that his problem-solving skills are above average. When the interviewer asked Jerry for evidence or examples that support his claim, he wasn't able to give specific data. He said things like, "Things come easy to me," or "I always know where to look," or "I just use my instincts." In response to the same question, another candidate stated, "Well, I was asked to serve on a task force for reducing the error rates on our processing procedure. I was also assigned as a mentor to help new hires solve problems. I also was asked to review the troubleshooting guide that the engineering staff developed for our unit." In the latter example, the evidence is specific and detailed.

Another important question asks the candidate to think about a time when he received feedback that he initially disagreed with and later came to accept. If the candidate addresses this question, it would be very helpful to determine how the candidate came to internalize the feedback. It shows that the candidate became open-minded at some point about the feedback. In reality, what often occurs is that people receive feedback that they don't agree with and then spend their time justifying their behavior or proving that the feedback is incorrect. Sometimes, indeed, the feedback is incorrect, but often it's not and we spend our time resisting what could help us.

FIGURE 3.1	Self-Awareness at a Glance	
	PROS	**CONS**
Impact on Others	• Aware that his behavior affects others • Recognizes his negative behavior • Willingly takes action to change his behavior • Can read nonverbal behavioral cues from others	• Blames his behavior on others • "Owns" no negative behavior • Expects others to accept his negative behavior • Struggles to identify nonverbal cues—even during the interview
Emotional and Inner Awareness	• Aware that her emotions exist and understands impact on behavior or performance • Can predict what triggers a negative reaction • Holds herself accountable when reflecting on behavior • Incorporates reflection as part of development • Uses reflection as a tool to determine how to modify future behavior	• Denies any connect between her emotions and behavior and performance • Lacks awareness of triggers or incidents that cause an emotional reaction • Fills self-reflection with blame, justification, minimizing wrong-doing, or denying responsibility • Is unable to self-reflect
Accurate Self-Assessment	• Able to list both strengths and weaknesses • Able to provide evidence of both	• Disputes feedback and does not examine behavior • Cannot provide any examples

(continued)

	PROS	CONS
FIGURE 3.1 *Continued*	strengths and weaknesses • Acknowledges feedback as valuable • Gives careful consideration of feedback from others • Gives examples of strengths in terms of performance • Gives examples of actions taken to improve weaknesses	• Sees evaluator as vindictive or ill informed • Dismisses feedback without consideration • When talking about strengths, has no sense of limitations • Unable to state strengths

Endnotes

1. Elizabeth J. Rozell, Charles E. Pettijohn, and R. Stephen Parker, "Emotional Intelligence and Dispositional Affectivity as Predictors of Performance in Salespeople," *Journal of Marketing Theory and Practice* (Spring 2006): 113.
2. D.R. Rhoades, K.F. MacFarland, and A.O. Johnson, "Speaking and Interruptions During Primary Care Office Visits," *Family Medicine* (July–August 2001): 528.
3. Ken Myers and Greg Herbert, "Dynamic Listening: An IT Manager's Key to Success with Staff, Customers and Clients," *IT Manager's Journal* (June 25, 2007), http://www.itmanagersjournal.com/feature/24834.
4. Kerry L. Johnson, "How to Gain Your Client's Trust—Fast," *CPA Journal* 63, 9 (September 1993): 40–42.
5. P. Russell, "Managing the Stress of Workplace Change," New Zealand Centre for Cognitive Behaviour Therapy, July 26, 2007, http://www.rational.org.nz/prof/docs/russell/changestress.htm.
6. Scott Beagrie and Justin McAvoy, "How to Handle Criticism," *Occupational Health* 59, 5 (May 2007): 24–25.
7. Nivedita Debnath and Kanika T. Bhal, "Polarization of Perceptions of IT-Enabled Privacy Violations at Workplace: Impact of Respondent Position,

Peer Belief and Peer Pressure," *Global Journal of Flexible Systems Management* (July–September 2003): 15.

8. Suzette Plaisance Bryan, "Emotional Intelligence and Intrapersonal Conversations," Consortium for Research on Emotional Intelligence in Organizations. *E-Journal: Issues and Recent Development in Emotional Intelligence.* August 20, 2007.

9. John J. Engels, " Delivering Difficult Messages," *Journal of Accountancy* 204, 1 (July 2007): 50.

10. Bryan, "Emotional Intelligence and Intrapersonal Conversations."

11. Adele B. Lynn, "A Quick Overview of Emotional Intelligence," *Hoosier Banker* 86, 5 (May 2002): 16.

12. A.W. Evans, R.M.A. Leeson, T.R.O. Newton John, and A. Petrie, "The Influence of Self-Deception and Impression Management upon Self-assessment in Oral Surgery," *British Dental Journal* (2005): 765–769.

13. Ibid.

14. Mathew Hayward, "Check Your Ego for Workplace Success," *Training and Development* 61, 3 (March 2007): 12.

15. David M. Herold, Donald B. Fedor, and Steven D. Caldwell, "Beyond Change Management: A Multilevel Investigation of Contextual and Personal Influences on Employees' Commitment to Change," *Journal of Applied Psychology* 92, 4 (July 2007): 942.

16. June I. Gravill, Deborah R. Compeau, and Barbara L. Marcolin, "Experience Effects on the Accuracy of Self-Assessed User Competence," *Information Management* 43, 2 (April 2006): 378.

CHAPTER 4

Self-Control or Self-Management

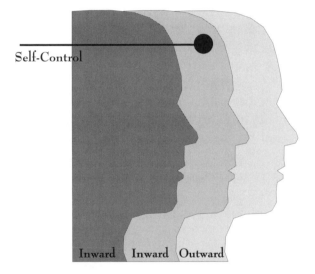

Self-Control

Inward   Inward   Outward

Competency 1—Emotional Expression
Competency 2—Courage or Assertiveness
Competency 3—Resilience
Competency 4—Planning the Tone of Conversations

Being aware of our emotions, our impact on others, and our strengths and weaknesses provides a great first step, but emotional intelligence by no means ends with self-awareness. Awareness of our impact on others begs the question, What, if anything, do we choose to do to control or manage our behavior? Self-control or self-management allows us to manage our frustrations, anger, fear, discouragement, and other emotions so that we achieve our goals and live our intentions. For example, if we become frustrated because of an obstacle at work and just give up on the goal, then we allow our emotions to thwart our intentions. What job doesn't have its share of frustrations? Who doesn't sometimes experience discouragement or defeat? How we react to and recover from such challenges separates the star performers from the ordinary performers.[1] If we allow our emotions to rob us of our intentions, then we function at less than full capacity.

Emotions can also hijack us from living the company values. Evidence of this appears in an article in *Canadian HR Reporter,* which states that anger is a threat to our corporate values because when executives lose control, they make the situation all about themselves and their anger, and they are no longer providing leadership to the company.[2] Marshall Goldsmith states it another way; he says, "When you get angry you are out of control. It's hard to lead people when you've lost control."[3] Leaders, however, are not the only concern. Employees who inappropriately express anger create hostile and abusive climates for their peers, resulting in more sick time, decreased productivity, and reduced organizational commitment.[4]

Self-control or self-management is characterized by four competencies:

1. *Emotional expression,* which means managing anger, stress, excitement, and frustration;

2. *Courage or assertiveness,* which means managing fear;

3. *Resilience,* which means managing disappointment, setbacks, or failure; and

4. *Planning the tone of conversations.*

Competency 1: Emotional Expression

Consider the very conscientious manager who wants everything in his department to be right. He also believes and articulates the company's value of treating people in a respectful manner. Yet, when someone puts a report on his desk containing errors, he gets so frustrated that he loses his temper and shouts, "I told you before that this report has to be right! Why can't you be more careful?" This manager may be very justified in his frustration, and certainly an error-free report is an admirable goal, but the manner in which he expressed his concern isn't likely to get a positive result.

Of course, self-management or self-control is important at all levels. The customer service representative who shouts at the customer, or the coworker whose sarcasm brings down her peers, or the production worker who withholds information for the next shift in an effort to "get even," all create disruptions. These expressions of verbal and nonverbal warfare affect morale as well as profits. Aggression, including harassment and bullying in the workplace, has become a growing concern in the United States. This behavior, which often has tacit acceptance, diminishes organizational performance. Workdays can be lost because of abuse, which can lead to errors, increased sick leave, and lost productivity.[5]

But make no mistake; anger by no means presents the only example of the need for better self-management or self-control. Another example occurs when a manager sits in a meeting reluctant to speak up about a new product rollout. His concern that he'll be labeled as a complainer if he voices his objections to the timetable renders him impotent. Yet, he knows that the timetable is unrealistic. This manager's fear of being labeled causes serious and important information to be withheld in the decision-making process. A manager with strong self-management skills controls or manages his fear in order to articulate his concerns for the common good of the company.

Another interesting example came from a large real estate development sales situation. The sales team leader, excited that he and his team were about to close on a $250 million project, was anxious to get it signed and tempted to just close the negotiations and wrap it up. However, he decided to manage his eagerness to close and just continue to listen. As he continued to listen to the clients, he was able to discern more of their needs. He added another $50 million to the project by managing his excitement and eagerness. And the clients felt that the solution better suited their long-term needs. Also, by spending the $50 million up front, the clients estimated that they saved more than $100 million they would have needed for future expansion.

So self-control or self-management leads to improvements in morale as well as profits. It allows people to reach goals and builds relationships. It encompasses all emotions. Having self-control or self-management means managing ourselves out of the rut, out of fear, out of anger, and out of disappointment, and motivates us to behave in a manner that helps us reach our goals and live our intentions.

When you couple self-awareness with self-control, you have a powerful combination that forms a strong foundation for emotional intelligence. Ascertaining whether the candidate has this foundation requires the interviewer or hiring manager to use a one-two approach in the interview questions. For example, in the self-awareness section, we suggested that you ask the candidate to tell you about some situations or people that annoy her in her present (or previous) position. In this example, the candidate should give the interviewer insight about her awareness of some of her triggers. By following that question with "Tell me what you did in those situations," the interviewer encourages the candidate to reveal her self-control or self-management skills.

Questions to Assess Appropriate Emotional Expression

Q: Describe some things that make you angry or frustrated at work.
  - Tell me what you do in those situations.

Q: Describe some types of situations where you are likely to get annoyed at work.
  - What do you do when you get annoyed?

Q: Tell me about a time when you were angry with someone at work.
  - What did you do?

Q: Has there ever been a situation at work where you said something and later regretted saying it?
- Tell me about that.

Q: Tell me about a time when you lost your temper at work.
- What did you do?
- What result did this have?

Q: Tell me about a time when you had too much to do at work and it was causing you to feel stressed.
- What did you do?

Q: What do you do when you are feeling stressed at work?

Q: Describe a stressful situation at work.
- What do you do?

Q: Describe a situation at work when you were very enthusiastic about something.
- How did your enthusiasm affect others?

Q: Describe a time when you felt excited about work.

Q: When do you look forward to going to work?

Q: Was there ever a time at work when you had to temper your enthusiasm for something?

Q: Describe a time when you felt grateful at work.
- What did you do?

Q: Give me an example of when you expressed gratitude toward someone at work.

KEY POINTS TO CONSIDER WHEN ASSESSING ANSWERS

We know that people's temperaments vary and that some people rarely get angry while others get excited easily. It's also important for you, the interviewer, to realize that your own temperament will influence your interpretation of the answers. If confrontation frightens you and the candidate states that she raised an issue with someone, you may judge this tactic as negative and confrontational. So, prior to asking these questions, determine the cultural and job fit. For example, what may be appropriate for one job may be inappropriate for another. Be sure to put the candidate at ease, or she may be reluctant to answer these questions in a straightforward manner.

Also, it's important for you, the interviewer, to realize that anger is not negative. How we express our anger, however, can be negative. So, focus your attention on the behavioral expression of the emotion. How did the candidate express her anger or frustration? Was it productive? Did the manner in which she addressed the situation maintain a positive working relationship with the other person? Were you able to gain evidence of this based on what the candidate told you? Look for constructive ways the candidate expressed herself. Some appropriate methods would include calling the person aside and discussing the situation, asking the person whether he would be willing to discuss alternative views, discussing the situation privately with a mentor to gain advice on how best to address it, taking a cooling-off or time-out period before addressing the situation, rethinking the perspective of the situation, or separating the event from the person. Remember: look for evidence from the candidate to indicate that she manages or expresses her anger or stress in an acceptable manner.

In this section, many of the questions assess anger or stress management. However, some questions ask about excitement, enthusiasm, and gratitude. Excitement, enthusiasm, and gratitude could be very positive qualities. The questions aimed at gauging these qualities help the interviewer to determine whether the candidate appropriately expresses emotion about work. Managing emotion doesn't mean that people shouldn't express emotion. Expressing positive feelings can generate a positive mood for others.[6] Positive feelings generate a contagious environment. Expressing enthusiasm, excitement, and gratitude can bond teams and create a positive workplace culture. People display these emotions in different ways. Some individuals may express enthusiasm quietly; others may be bubbly. The point of these questions is to determine whether the candidate recognizes and behaves in a manner that allows for positive expression of emotions. The question about tempering enthusiasm is an important one. A good example came from a candidate excited about a promotion that he received. He said that he knew that a coworker interviewed for the promotion and did not get the position. He said that he carefully decided not to "rub it in his face" because he knew his coworker was disappointed. He also approached the coworker and discussed the issue. The candidate's sensitivity about the issue and his behavior demonstrated his awareness of the impact of expressing emotions.

Competency 2: Courage or Assertiveness

Courage in business seldom resembles the heroic impulsiveness that sometimes surfaces in life-and-death situations.[7] However, courage to speak the truth, to challenge popular opinion, to say no when everyone else is saying yes, or to challenge a coworker who is taking shortcuts that put the organization at risk is a commodity in organizations that sometimes seems to be in short supply. Yet, when people exercise courage and speak up about coworkers' behavior or about broken processes, not only does job satisfaction improve, but the system is also improved.[8] Courage is defined as taking calculated risks to speak up about workplace issues, goals, and concerns that affect the organization, customer, patient, or product and doing so in a productive manner. We're not talking about a bank teller refusing to hand over the cash at gunpoint. Instead, we want to determine whether people have the necessary courage and skill to voice counter opinions, to challenge the status quo, and to have difficult conversations. No one relishes an uncomfortable conversation, but sidestepping tough discussions can leave important issues unaddressed, creating even bigger problems.[9]

For leaders and managers, addressing performance or conduct problems is an essential part of the job. Yet, many managers dislike and avoid this task. In "The Managerial Moment of Truth: The Essential Step in Helping People Improve Performance," authors Bruce Bodaken and Robert Fritz state that the inherent awkwardness of evaluating an employee's performance may cause managers to avoid confrontation altogether, resulting in work not done right, tension among employees, and unnecessary strain on high performers.[10] In management and leadership ranks, these conversations must take place. Confronting performance problems and addressing concerns with peers are also part of the job. Yet, here again, avoidance often rules. Avoidance is all about fear.[11] When people do exhibit courage at work, they find a direct correlation between courage and success.[12]

A candidate's courage should be examined for motive and method. By asking the candidate why he decided to speak up about a particular issue at a particular time, you will gain insight into the motivation behind the courage. Is the person someone who feels anointed to take other people's issues as his own? Does he regularly fight injustice? Is the person concerned about saving face? Is his motive to protect himself? Is he speaking up because he is concerned that someone else may state his case incorrectly? Or is he speaking up to gain favor? By asking the question, the interviewer encourages the candidate to reveal information useful to the decision-making process. Assessing method also proves useful. Does the candidate speak up in a straightforward manner that engenders trust? Or does the candidate employ methods that are more divisive? Also, in what tone does the candidate speak his mind? How does he frame his issue?

Questions to Assess Courage or Assertiveness

Q: Tell me about a time when you spoke up about something in the workplace.
  - What was the issue?
  - Why did you speak up about it?
  - What did you say?
  - What did others think?

Q: Has there ever been a situation at work where you wish you had said something in a meeting or encounter but didn't?
  - Tell me about that.

Q: Describe what you did the last time someone blamed you for something at work that wasn't your fault.
  - What did you do?

Q: Describe a time when you were right and you knew you were right, but the other party (customer, coworker, your boss) at work didn't believe you.
  - What did you do?

Q: Tell me about a time when you felt something was unfair at work.
 • What did you do?

Q: Tell me about a time when you knew that you were told to do something that you thought wasn't a good idea.
 • What did you do?

For managers or leaders:

Q: Tell me about a time when you disagreed about the direction of the company or a policy.
 • What did you do?

Q: Describe a time when you and a peer were at odds about a particular decision or direction.
 • What did you do?

Q: Tell me about a time when your boss had a particular opinion that differed from yours.
 • What did you do?

Q: Tell me about a time when you disagreed with a goal that you were told to achieve.
 • How did that go?

Q: Describe a difficult performance discussion that you had with an employee.

Q: Tell me about a time when you decided not to discuss an issue with an employee.
 • What did you consider?

KEY POINTS TO CONSIDER WHEN ASSESSING ANSWERS

Courage to speak up when appropriate engenders many fine qualities. Of course, recognizing how and when to speak up and when it's best to let things go depends on the person's role and the situation. Getting into an argument with a customer over who is right may be a huge waste of time and drive the customer away. However, speaking out about what is right if you're the CFO may be a critical job function. Obviously, then, accurate analysis of the answers to these questions requires filtering them through both the job function and the situation. In advance of the interview, you'll want to build the case for when these competencies are important. In general, though, you'll be assessing a candidate's likelihood of speaking up and doing so in a productive manner rather than being paralyzed by fear or inertia. Generally, these questions form an interesting balance with the questions about anger management. Usually, temperament forces people to be on one side or the other—either too assertive or not assertive enough. You're not trying to change the person's basic temperament, but rather determine his or her basic tendency and how he uses past experience to know how to navigate these situations. Look for answers that demonstrate that the candidate understand his basic tendencies and has taken steps to either turn up or turn down the volume on his assertiveness so that his behaviors produce the desired results with others. Also, you can determine whether the candidate has the courage to take responsibility for his environment by bringing up situations that could be improved. You can also determine if the candidate will contribute ideas and suggestions or just go along with the status quo.

In a management or leadership candidate, look for excuses. Some people say they don't confront negative behavior because they know the organization won't back them, or because they don't want to hurt someone's feelings, or because others will decrease productivity, or because the timing wasn't right. Be on the lookout for answers that suggest that the candidate skirts issues.

Follow-up questions that consider motive provide another layer of information. Ask, "Why did you decide to speak up?" or "Why did you consider this issue important?" or "Why did you decide not to speak up?" Again, you'll need to assess the answers by taking into consideration the job function and the culture of the organization.

Competency 3: Resilience

The extent to which we keep our spirits up when things do not work out as we would have liked is resilience. Resilience means that we keep trying, even when we face obstacles. Resilience means that when one door closes, we look for another door. Resilience means that we look for lessons learned when something doesn't work out. Resilience means that we don't give up. Some highly resilient people use failure as a launching board. They view failure as information to help them succeed at their next attempt. People high in career resilience see themselves as competent individuals who control their responses to what happens to them. They respond to obstacles and undesired events by reframing their ideas and repositioning their energies to allow them to move ahead anyway.[13] When people lack resilience or optimism about achieving goals, indeed, they are less likely to achieve them.[14] Personal resilience also leads to higher levels of change acceptance.[15]

On the contrary, people with low resilience have difficulty bouncing back from setbacks. Setbacks may paralyze or even kill any motivation to set or reach future goals. These people may change only when change is thrust upon them as the last or only alternative. People with low resilience often feel victimized by situations and express powerlessness over their future. Consider Jon, who had been unemployed for more than three years due to a downsizing. He said that he hasn't been actively looking for a job because he knows the job market is weak in his field and that he knows of many people who are in the same boat. He said that he doubts he'll ever recover and get a job like the one he once had. He refused company outplacement services and also turned down some retraining money. A sense of hopelessness surrounds him. As an interviewer or hiring manager, you probably won't have to worry about Jon, because he won't even apply for the jobs your company has to offer. But be on the lookout for less obvious cases.

Maria, on the contrary, also suffered through downsizing. Although financially the situation presented a significant challenge, she decided to view this experience as an opportunity to gain some new skills. She took advantage of company and government retraining dollars. She also worked part-time at a minimum-wage job to make ends meet. Now she is excited and delighted about her future opportunities in her new field. She conveys in the interview that being downsized was the best thing that ever happened to her. She convinces the interviewer that she is passionate and eager to make a contribution. She gets the job! Maria did not give up, and that resilience came through in her behaviors following the downsizing.

Q: Tell me about a time when you felt that you were defeated at work.
  • What did you do?

Q: Tell me about a time when you were distracted or preoccupied about something.
  • What did you do?

Q: Tell me about a time when you felt like giving up on something.
  • What did you do?

Q: Describe a time when you didn't think things could get any worse, and then they did.
  • What did you do?

Q: Tell me about a time when you decided to give up on a goal.

Q: Tell me about a time when you were overwhelmed at your last job.
  • How often does that occur?
  • What do you do about it?

Q: Talk about the last time you were criticized at work.
  • How did that go?

KEY POINTS TO CONSIDER WHEN ASSESSING ANSWERS

For most of us, life just isn't rosy all the time. By asking people to assess how they react to those times when work gets discouraging or when they feel overwhelmed indicates how resilient a person is during the difficult times. In response to questions about these situations, most people will want to filter their answers to present only a positive picture, so setting the tone for an honest discussion is important. You can do this by stating, "We know that every day can't be a great day; I'd like to know more about those days at work that don't go so well." Then listen for the candidate's ability to bounce back. First, what alerts the candidate to his response to bad days? Then, does the candidate have some sort of system to recover or cope with the bad days? If possible, it would also be useful to assess how many of these days the person encounters. (If every day is a bad day, that may be cause for concern.)

Be sure to look for the methods people use to overcome obstacles. It's not that resilient people don't have bad days, but they create ways to get through them. Oftentimes, resilient people realize that the situation is temporary. Others say they put the situation in perspective. Some say they talk it over with a confidant and realize that they may be blowing things out of proportion. Still others talk about what they may have been able to learn from these kinds of experiences. Candidates who dwell on the situations, place blame, constantly run away from challenging situations, give up, or describe victim or powerlessness behaviors provide the interviewer with cause for concern.

BONUS QUESTIONS: AWARENESS AND CONTROL IN THE MOMENT

An important concept in emotional intelligence requires people to be able to exercise both self-awareness and self-control "in the moment." By exercising self-awareness and self-control in the moment, we avoid backtracking, hurt feelings, and wasted communication. For example, realizing after the fact that an action or behavior caused harm or was inappropriate proves better than not being aware at all, but it still requires the person to go back and right the situation. Perhaps the situation required an apology, or a discussion to clear the air. One manager summed it up by stating that she thought about how she treated a particular employee and realized that she lacked patience in the situation. She decided to apologize to the employee and then set aside time to listen to the employee's issue.

However, if a person can recognize and exercise self-awareness and self-control as the situation unfolds, she can then choose to act in an appropriate manner, thus eliminating unnecessary turmoil or backtracking. If the manager in the example in the last paragraph realized that her impatience affected the way she interacted with the employee, she could have adjusted her behavior on the spot. Interviewers and hiring managers should assess whether a candidate is aware and adjusts her behavior in the moment.

Q: Tell me about a time when you realized that a conversation wasn't going very well. (Is the candidate able to realize during the situation the dynamics of the situation?)

- What did you do? (Is the candidate able to redirect the conversation for a better outcome?)

Q: Tell me about a time when you realized that you weren't speaking up during a meeting.

- What did you do?

Q: Tell me about a time when you realized that something was best left unsaid.

- What did you do?

KEY POINTS TO CONSIDER WHEN ASSESSING ANSWERS

When exercising emotional intelligence in the moment, a person chooses to redirect conversations or actions as they unfold. The interviewer should look for examples where the candidate states that *during* a conversation or encounter, she steered the conversation in a more productive direction. Although it may prove difficult for the candidate to come up with examples, these kinds of displays of emotional intelligence speak volumes. A typical example might be: "The other day I was on the telephone asking for some information from a peer in another department. The peer, in a curt voice, said she didn't have time to give me the information. I was annoyed at her answer, but immediately I thought, it isn't going to get me anywhere to be curt in return. Therefore, I thought about her situation and I said, 'I realize it's the end of the month and you're probably swamped. In fact, I hate to bother you with this request when I know you have so many other things to do.' She's a very reasonable person, so she said, 'I'm sorry. I really am swamped and we're shorthanded today. I know you need this. I can get this to you after lunch. Would that be okay?' " This candidate was able to give a concrete example of a time when she took steps to exercise emotional intelligence during the encounter that resulted in a more positive outcome. Had she acted on the fact that she was annoyed at being put off by her peer, she could have escalated the conflict. To establish awareness in the moment, look for evidence of both restraint in escalating conflict and also examples of having the courage to speak up when appropriate. Both factors contribute to successful interactions.

Competency 4: Planning the Tone of Conversations

In addition to being aware in the moment, emotionally intelligent people take this skill a step further by planning the tone of their conversations so that they achieve the best results. To preplan a conversation or tone of a conversation, a person must anticipate reactions, impact, and outcomes. For example, the physician who curtly announces that you have less than six months to live and then walks out to attend to the next patient isn't demonstrating much emotional intelligence. Likewise, the salesperson who fails to establish rapport or doesn't anticipate or ask about a client's needs hasn't planned the conversation or tone that will achieve the best result. We're talking not about a rote script, but rather about true awareness and skill at setting tone and strategy so that the best outcomes follow.

Questions to Assess Planning Tone

Q: Tell me about a time when you deliberately planned the tone of a particular conversation. (This indicates that the candidate is aware that tone affects outcome.)
  - How did you do that? (This indicates skill.)
  - What result did it have?

Q: In your present job, can you tell me about some situations when you must think about how you are going to say something before saying it?
  - What must you consider?

Q: Tell me about a time when you planned the way you phrased a problem or situation so that you could get the best result.

Q: Tell me about a time when you missed an opportunity to set the tone in a discussion.
  - What happened?

KEY POINTS TO CONSIDER WHEN ASSESSING ANSWERS

Just as strategy factors into business success, strategy also factors into our success in our human relationships. By strategizing to get the best outcome from a conversation, a person deliberately determines how to interact in a productive manner. When the candidate answers these questions, the interviewer should look for how the candidate planned and prepared for the conversation by anticipating the reactions of the other party. For example, the candidate may relay a situation similar to the following: "I had to talk to a coworker about a problematic situation. Earlier, we had a staff meeting and decided on several actions that we could take to help one another meet the end-of-day cutoff deadline for running work. The coworker wasn't doing something that we agreed to at our staff meeting and it was affecting my results. I thought about how he might react. I anticipated that he could get defensive when I approached him. So, I decided to open the conversation by saying that several of the actions he was taking as a result of our staff meeting were really helping me meet my deadlines, and I thanked him for that. I asked if things were okay from his perspective, regarding the new actions. Then I broached the subject of the problem. I'm so glad I decided to think about how to approach him, because he was very open to talking about the problem. If I had just come out and accused him of not doing something we agreed to, he would have had a very negative reaction." In this example, the interviewer can see that the candidate was sensitive to the fact that he could set the tone of the discussion by the way he approached his coworker. The candidate gave forethought to his strategy and delivered it in a way that achieved a positive result.

Of course, this skill always has the potential for abuse. If a person sets the tone with the goal of creating outcomes that benefit only her or if she uses an insincere tone, she can be considered manipulative. Asking candidates to fully describe the situation or outcomes allows for a fuller disclosure of the facts. Also, probing questions about motive clarify the candidate's intentions and sincerity. One candidate seeking approval of the lead engineer said, "I knew if I buttered George up, I'd get his approval for the project and I'd look like a hero to the guys upstairs." Although this candidate may be sincere, further probing is in order because at face value, this response sounds quite manipulative. Also, the candidate's motives seem corrupt. A more in-depth discussion of manipulation and other warning signs for interviewers and hiring managers follows in the last chapter of this book.

	FIGURE 4.1 Self-Control or Self-Management at a Glance	
	PROS	**CONS**
Emotional Expression	• Expresses emotion with impact on others in mind • Tempers enthusiasm (if necessary) to show sensitivity toward others • Expresses anger in a constructive manner • Gives examples of expressing thanks and gratitude toward others	• Claims he never expresses or feels negative • Too readily expresses anger • Behaves inappropriately when angry (especially without remorse or regret) • When overwhelmed or stressed, takes it out on others
Courage or Assertiveness	• Is able to take actions on issues of importance • Takes actions when work or organization is at risk • Is able to recognize when an issue is worth challenging • Does not let fear immobilize her or mute her position • Can give examples of exercising judgment while taking risk	• Is unable to separate the issues; lacks perspective on which issues require courage and which require letting go • Is unable to see the need for compromise • Goes along too readily with status quo despite misgivings • Can't provide example of speaking up about something important

(continued)

FIGURE 4.1 *Continued*		
	PROS	**CONS**
Resilience	• Gives examples of learning from failure or criticism • Accepts challenges or obstacles and seeks solutions • Can articulate coping mechanisms for negative circumstances • Takes responsibility for actions to create a better situation when faced with obstacles • Reframes a negative situation to look for opportunities • Relies on inner strength to deal with negative situations	• Is unable to give an example of over-coming a failure • When facing criticism, gives up • Lacks confidants or appropriate coping mechanisms to assist with negative circumstances • Places blame on others for negative situations • Appears powerless or victimized when describing negative situations

Endnotes

1. Robert E. Kelley, *How to Be a Star at Work* (New York: Times Business, Random House, 1998).
2. Todd Humber, "Emotional Intelligence," *Canadian HR Reporter* 15, 16 (2002): G1.
3. Marshall Goldsmith, "Which Workplace Habits Do You Need to Break to Become More Successful?" *Journal for Quality and Participation* 30, 2 (Summer 2007): 4.
4. C.M. Pearson, L.M. Andersson, and C.L. Porath, "Assessing and Attacking Workplace Incivility," *Organizational Dynamics* 29 (2000): 123–37.
5. Diane Bandow and Debra Hunter, "The Rise of Workplace Incivilities: Has It Happened to You?" *Business Review* (Summer 2007): 212.
6. Sigal G. Barsade, "The Ripple Effect: Emotional Contagion and Its Influence on Group Behavior," *Administrative Science Quarterly* 47 (December 2002): 644.

7. Kathleen K. Reardon, "Courage as a Skill," *Harvard Business Review* 85, 1 (2007): 58.
8. D. Maxfield, J. Grenny, R. McMillan, K. Patterson, and A. Switzler, "Silence Kills," *VitalSmarts* (2005): 9.
9. John J. Engels, "Delivering Difficult Messages," *Journal of Accountancy* 204, 1 (July 2007): 50.
10. Bruce Bodaken and Robert Fritz, "The Managerial Moment of Truth: The Essential Step in Helping People Improve Performance," *Publishers Weekly,* March 20, 2006, 47.
11. Engels, "Delivering Difficult Messages."
12. Sandra Ford Walston, "Things to Love About Courage," *Strategic Finance* 89, 1 (July 2007): 17.
13. Jane Goodman, "Career Adaptability in Adults: A Construct Whose Time Has Come," *Career Development Quarterly* 43, 1 (September 1994): 74.
14. Christopher Peterson and Martin E.P. Seligman, *Character Strengths and Virtues* (New York: Oxford University Press, 2004).
15. Connie R. Wanberg and Joseph T. Banas, "Predictors and Outcomes of Openness to Changes in a Reorganizing Workplace," *Journal of Applied Psychology* 85, 1 (February 2000): 132.

CHAPTER 5

Empathy

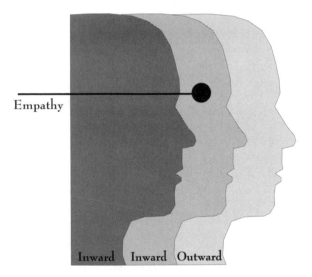

Empathy

Inward   Inward   Outward

Competency 1—Respectful Listening
Competency 2—Feeling the Impact on Others
Competency 3—Service Orientation

E mpathy, which is the ability to understand the perspective of others, constitutes the second area of emotional intelligence. Empathy is characterized by three competencies:

1. *Respectful listening,* which is the ability to give careful and respectful attention to others;

2. *Feeling the impact on others,* which is the ability to assess and determine how situations as well as our words and actions affect others; and

3. *Service orientation,* which is the desire to help others.

Competency 1: Respectful Listening

Empathy requires us to respectfully listen to others. Respectfully listening means that we're listening with the purpose of understanding. Too often, we listen for the purpose of refuting or building our own case. Respectful listening is especially important when we disagree with someone or when we are in a conflict situation. Through respectful listening we are able to develop a deep understanding of what the other person's point of view may be. A deep understanding enables us to comprehend the underlying issues, values, and feelings associated with the other person's position. Marshall Goldsmith described not listening as the most passive-aggressive form of disrespect for colleagues.[1]

Consider the customer service worker unable to understand the perspective of an angry customer. If the customer service representative is without empathy, the conflict generally escalates. When the worker expresses empathy, the angry customer often calms down. A simple, sincere response, such as, "I'm sorry you're having this problem and I'd like to work with you to solve it. May I have your account number?" changes the complexion of the interaction. Instead, however, many customer service personnel robotically ask, "Account number?" Sure, their intention may be good. They can't look into the situation without an account number, but their lack of expressed empathy may just infuriate a customer.

Q: Think about a time when you didn't understand something in the workplace.

- What did you do?

Q: Describe a situation when you didn't understand why someone was acting a certain way or taking a certain position on some issue.

- What did you do?

Q: Describe a time when you jumped to conclusions.

Q: Tell me about a conversation with a coworker, employee, or customer that didn't go very well.

- What specifically occurred?

For managers or leaders:

Q: Tell me about a time when you learned something by listening to an employee.

Q: Describe a time when you asked someone for information about a problem.

KEY POINTS TO CONSIDER WHEN ASSESSING ANSWERS

Listening skills have many different levels of competency. Listening to gain information helps the candidate learn something. The candidate should be able to give examples when she asked clarifying questions, probed, or otherwise asked questions, and then listened to the answers to discern information. Listening for information provides payoffs in terms of quality and costs. According to an article in *Quality Progress,* two case studies presented clear evidence that listening to workers can result in big payback opportunities, which in turn result in cost and quality improvements.[2] Fundamental to the entire quality movement is the idea that solutions to problems come from listening to the people who are closest to the work. Obviously, managers and leaders should demonstrate in the interview process that they listen to information from a wide variety of sources.

The next level of listening requires the candidate to give examples of how he sought to understand someone's position or actions that were different from his own. In these examples, the candidate should give examples of how listening helped him better understand the underlying issues, values, or feelings associated with another person's position. Watch for the candidate's summary of this situation. Does he end it with, "I still can't understand how someone could take such a position." Or did the candidate walk away with a better and deeper understanding? He may still disagree with the other person's position, but he may demonstrate a different attitude about the person and his views. Also, watch for a respectful tone during the description of the encounter. If the candidate describes a situation in a tone that is incredulous of the other person's beliefs or actions, you can bet that the same tone comes across in his encounters with others. He's probably not listening to understand, but rather listening to prove his point.

Asking for contrary evidence always adds a deeper dimension to the interview process. By asking about times when a candidate jumped to conclusions or when a conversation didn't go very well, the interviewer gains important information about self-awareness and the reflection methods the candidate employs in the area of listening.

Competency 2: Feeling the Impact on Others

Empathy also means that we can "feel" the impact of situations and understand how our words and actions affect others. Our ability to feel the impact of situations and of our behaviors and words on others generates a strong foundation to build relationships. Knowing on this level means that we know not because someone has told us; instead, we know because we have compassion for the other person's situation or experience. The coworker who recognizes the signs of an overwhelmed peer, the manager who can "see" the employee who struggles, and the leader who recognizes that the turmoil of change causes stress on the workforce all experience empathy. What they do next, however, separates those who only see from those who know how to skillfully express concern. Skillful expression of empathy depends on the person's role. We're not advocating that managers rescue people or loosen standards or that leaders forgo change because of the stress it creates. Instead, appropriately responding and allowing dialogue to occur recognize and honor the person who is struggling.

Questions to Assess Feeling the Impact on Others

Q: Tell me about a situation when you sensed something was bothering a peer or coworker.
- How did you know?
- What did you do?

Q: Describe a situation when you knew that something was wrong with a relationship you had with a peer, customer, or supervisor.
- What did you do?

Q: Relate a situation in which you determined that something that you did or said didn't go over very well.
- How did you know?

Q: Describe a time when you said or did something that had a negative effect on someone.

Q: Describe a time when you did or said something that had a negative effect on someone and you were unaware of it until someone else brought it to your attention.

For managers or leaders:

Q: Tell me about a time when you sensed that an employee was struggling.
- How did you know?
- What did you do?

Q: Tell me about a time when you noticed that your staff was overwhelmed.
- How did you know?
- What did you do?

Q: Describe a time when a change you were implementing caused stress for your staff.
- How did you know?
- What did you do?

KEY POINTS TO CONSIDER WHEN ASSESSING ANSWERS

Look for empathy that emanates from within the candidate. If we must rely on others to bring to our attention occurrences that require empathy, then the effectiveness of our interactions diminishes. Did the candidate's understanding come from within? During the interview process, these questions can help you determine whether the candidate understands, expresses, or displays empathy toward others. Look for evidence that the candidate reads nonverbal cues, notices nuances or differences in people's behavior, or otherwise recognizes cues that indicate that something was amiss. Then assess the candidate's actions. Did she approach the person? Did she choose to ignore the behavior? Did she open dialogue? Did she lower standards or expectations? Did she rescue the person? (More information about expressed empathy appears in the next section, "Service Orientation—Desire to Help Others.")

One candidate who noticed that a coworker was stressed by some recent software changes said that he wrote a fake memo from the head of the IT department stating that the software was going to be discontinued because it was difficult to use. This candidate was quite capable of reading the situation but failed sharply when it came to expressing empathy. Needless to say, his actions caused even more harm. They also violated just about every work rule imaginable. Sometimes the answers you get to these questions will amaze you!

The person who is well meaning but unable to understand his impact may well fall short of the requirements for a job that requires interactions with others. Assess the person's level of awareness and how in tune he is with how others are experiencing him. If a candidate struggles to come up with an answer to these questions, he may lack empathy and be unable to recognize the plight of others.

Competency 3: Service Orientation

Empathy leads to a desire to help others. This desire to be of service, or service orientation, fosters helpful behaviors toward customers, coworkers, and others. With empathy present in our relationships, we orient ourselves toward helping one another. This service orientation or desire to help others is particularly useful in the workplace. According to New York restaurateur Danny Meyer's recently published book, *Setting the Table: The Transforming Power of Hospitality in Business,* "emotional hospitality" (which emanates directly from empathy) is the distinguishing factor for success in any service business.[3] Most positions, regardless of the level, job function, or industry, require some level of service orientation toward either internal or external customers. However, empathy as a core competency reaches far beyond the service industry. Without empathy, influence is not possible.[4] Empathy is an essential building block in influencing others.[5] Great leaders must be able to understand and be empathetic to each person they work with.[6] Empathy, then, becomes critical for anyone in a leadership position.

Empathy comes into play, for example, when peers work in a team environment. Teammates often have both common and individual goals to achieve. Empathy enables teammates to understand one another's workloads and contributes to service-type behaviors. If a teammate can empathize with a peer, then that teammate can act accordingly. Appropriate behavior might include offering help or resources, aiding in problem solving, or assisting in some other way to get the job done. In one example, the director of manufacturing was particularly short staffed due to technical changes on the production line, and a backup resulted. The engineering director, without being asked, offered staff resources, thus enabling the company to meet the tight production schedule. Of course, this kind of assistance can be mandated, but when it occurs because of empathy, the teamwork atmosphere extends to others and serves as an example as well.

In another example, a building janitor was able to see that a guest appeared confused. He asked if he could be of help and took the guest to the correct elevator tower. This simple gesture required empathy on the part of the janitor. He could have missed the cues or simply not cared about the guest's dilemma.

The janitor demonstrated a service orientation toward the guest. When service orientation is born out of empathy rather than job duty, you have found the kind of employee who naturally wants to be helpful. It's relatively easy to teach someone how to be helpful. It's much more difficult to teach someone to *want* to be helpful. A recent study in *Personnel Psychology* indicated that people who had a high positive affectivity disposition were more likely to provide help and support in the workplace. High positive affectivity describes individuals who tend to be cheerful and energetic, and who experience positive moods, across a variety of situations, as compared to individuals who tend to be low energy and sluggish or melancholy. Regardless of gender or level of management responsibility, this quality produced greater service orientation than any other.[7] Hiring for service orientation is an important competency in many positions.

Questions to Assess Service Orientation

Q: Tell me about a time when you offered assistance to someone without being asked.
  - What did you do?

Q: Describe a situation when you offered assistance to someone even though it was outside of your job description.
  - What did you do?

Q: Relate an instance when someone needed help and you couldn't help him.
  - What did you do?

Q: Tell me about a time when you recognized that someone needed help.
  - What did you do?

Q: Describe a situation when you were asked to help someone at work.
  - What did you think about that?

Q: Was there ever a time when you resented helping someone at work?
  - Tell me about that.

For the manager or leader:

Q: Tell me about a time when an employee was struggling.
  - What did you do?

KEY POINTS TO CONSIDER WHEN ASSESSING ANSWERS

As we said earlier, service orientation is important. In this series of questions, the interviewer should be determining whether the candidate is helpful without being asked. First, is the candidate able to see the need? Second, is the candidate willing to assist? The interviewer will be able to determine this by how readily the candidate can come up with concrete examples of when she offered assistance to others. Look for a wide variety of examples. In other words, did the candidate help coworkers? How about peers from other departments? Also look for the candidate's willingness to assist outside her job description. Even a small thing like the example of the janitor offering directions without being asked, is an example of a person assisting others outside his job description. It's also telling when a person can determine that someone is struggling or confused and then offers assistance accordingly. Someone who is service oriented yet unable to directly assist another person will often serve as a broker or conduit for the person needing assistance. In other words, the service-oriented individual will make a phone call or introduce someone who can help the person in need, or will direct the person to someone who will know the answer. People who are service oriented can't always solve a problem, but they are concerned enough about a person who needs help to direct her to someone who can.

There are a few cautions to consider when evaluating service orientation. The interviewer will need to determine whether the candidate is aware of when he is being taken advantage of by a "needy" coworker, someone who always seems to need help. This kind of manipulation on the part of the coworker can be particularly challenging for someone with a strong service orientation. There is a fine line between being helpful and being used—although to err on the side of being helpful is preferred. That's why the question about whether or not the candidate has ever resented helping someone is important. It will give the interviewer an idea about how the candidate balances these points.

Another caution applies to managers or leaders who display rescuing behavior. Rescuing behavior results when compassion for an employee who is struggling causes the manager to lower or compromise standards. The manager may also give the work to other more capable people to cover for the employee who is struggling. Being empathic toward employees who are struggling does not mean that a manager should forgo standard performance-management techniques. On the contrary, empathy should serve as an entrée to the performance-management discussion. Empathy will also enable the manager to build rapport with the struggling employee, thus building a bridge for better performance.

FIGURE 5.1 **Empathy at a Glance**		
	PRO	**CON**
Respectful Listening	• Answers demonstrate he uses listening to value others • Willingly seeks others' thoughts to deepen understanding • Uses listening as a means to learn • Reacts to nonverbal cues to further understanding or listening	• Does not listen during the interview • Uses listening as a weapon to further her point • Doesn't recognize nonverbal cues during the interview • Isn't able to give examples of listening to understand or gain information
Feeling Impact on Others	• Readily gives examples of understanding how situations affect others • Gives examples of recognizing views or opinions of others even when she disagrees • Talks about self in terms that are relative to others • Uses active listening to ascertain the feelings of others	• Is unable to recognize a person's reactions to his behavior • Dismisses impact or feelings of others as irrelevant • Has difficulty thinking in terms of others; instead talks about me, me, me • Is unable to recognize how someone is viewing a particular situation

	PRO	CON
Service Orientation	• Can readily give an example of when he noticed the needs of others • Demonstrates action that responds to needs of others • Can give examples of helping others even outside of his job description • Points others in the direction of help if she is unable to help the person • Offers suggestions or solutions to those in need of assistance	• Is blind to or unable to give examples of recognizing the needs of others • Devalues the needs of others • Is unable to give concrete examples of actions that helped others • Talks in vague generalities about helping others • Puts his own needs and work before the needs of others

FIGURE 5.1 *Continued*

Endnotes

1. Marshall Goldsmith, "Which Workplace Habits Do You Need to Break to Become More Successful?" *Journal for Quality and Participation* 30, 2 (Summer 2007): 4.
2. Harry P. Richard, "Listen to the Workers," *Quality Progress* 33, 12 (December 2000): 136.
3. D. Meyer, "'51-Percenters' Have Five Key Emotional Skills Necessary to Provide Excellent Hospitality," *Nation's Restaurant News* 41, 6 (February 2007): 14.
4. Svetlana Holt and Steve Jones, "Emotional Intelligence and Organizational Performance: Implications for Performance Consultants and Educators," *Performance Improvement* 44, 10 (November–December 2005): 15.
5. Adele B. Lynn, *The EQ Difference* (New York: AMACOM, 2004).
6. Michael Kinsman, "Workplace Success Often Is Tied to Social Intelligence," *Knight Ridder Tribune Business News,* February 26, 2006, 1.

7. Ginka Toegel, N. Anand, and Martin Kilduff, "Emotion Helpers: The Role of High Positive Affectivity and High Self-Monitoring Managers," *Personnel Psychology* 60, 2 (Summer 2007): 337.

CHAPTER 6

Social Expertness

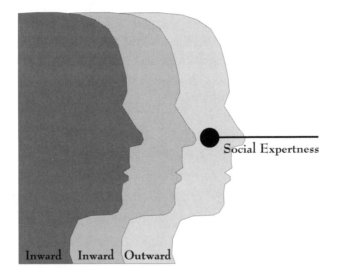

Inward   Inward   Outward

Social Expertness

Competency 1—Building Relationships
Competency 2—Collaboration
Competency 3—Conflict Resolution
Competency 4—Organizational Savvy

Social expertness is the ability to build genuine relationships and bonds and express caring, concern, and conflict in healthy ways. It includes four competencies:

1. *Building relationships,* which is the ability to build social bonds with others;

2. *Collaboration,* which is the ability to invite others in and value their thoughts related to ideas, projects, and work;

3. *Conflict resolution,* which is the ability to resolve differences; and

4. *Organizational savvy,* which is the ability to understand and maneuver within organizations.

Being adept at building and sustaining relationships leads to star performance within organizations.[1] When all other factors are equal, how we manage our relationships is the distinguishing factor that defines success. The ability to build honorable relationships and relate interpersonally is of critical importance to many job functions. The more a job requires cross-departmental and/or peer interactions, the more important building honorable relationships becomes. Also, as people move up the corporate ladder, the need to develop enterprisewide solutions requires interactions with peers and others. The quality of those interactions will often lead to the best solutions. When those interactions are laced with collaboration, even greater synergy and teamwork result. Those at the top of their performance look for and create opportunities and invite collaboration. Those who fail often don't recognize the value of creating strong collaborative relationships. In fact, research from the Center for Creative Leadership suggests that the reasons executives fail are related to interpersonal failures, not failures of technical competence.[2]

Beyond collaboration, top performers know that conflicts are inevitable. So, as they build a solid foundation with peers and others, they know that those relationships will be able to withstand the strains of conflict. They know that expressing conflict or differences in a way that maintains and preserves the integrity of the relationship will lead to better results. So the ability to build genuine relationships and bonds and express caring, concern, and conflict in healthy ways is critical to success in many jobs.

Star performers also know how to advance ideas within organizations, gain sponsors, and maneuver in complex organizations. They recognize that organizational savvy is a required skill for getting results within organizations. These competencies are all demonstrated within the confines of social expertness. Of course, the interviewer or hiring manager must determine which job functions within the organization require these skills. Some job functions require these skills to a much greater degree than others.

Consider the accounting analyst who needs data from several departments in order to complete the month-end report. Her requests may fall on deaf ears if she approaches people only when she needs something, doesn't bother to reciprocate, or uses a demanding tone. However, if she has taken time to build a rapport with and establish a genuine interest in the people she must interact with, those people are more likely to respond favorably to her requests. It's also important that she respect and reciprocate when others require assistance.

The director who was responsible for implementing an organizationwide IT system provides another example. Standard procedure included discussing needs with users, responding to user ideas and suggestions, communicating project status, and delivering effective user training and interface. But what the director did behind the scenes was also critical. She had well-established working relationships with all the other department heads, who knew that she listened to their needs and responded appropriately. The trust she had built over the years was a critical factor in the success of the project. Many other IT directors follow the same steps, but their projects are met with resistance. The difference often comes down to the relationships that managers build.

In yet another example, a creative engineer decided that he wanted to leave his present position; he was frustrated because no one would listen to his ideas. The engineer had some great ideas, but he tended to present them in an arrogant manner. His usual approach was to open with a sarcastic remark that belittled the current system or project. He then proceeded to argue his idea, stating that it was of course better than the current system. His peers and even his boss felt that he was attacking their previous efforts, so they didn't support him. His ideas generally fell flat because he couldn't get others to buy into them. Most organizations don't automatically respond to ideas; ideas must be sold.

If an employee doesn't understand that dynamic and have the skill to gain support, he may feel as though his talents are wasted.

Social expertness comes down to very simple things. One person said that she purposely withholds information from a coworker because the coworker talks to her only when she needs something. You might argue that both are immature and should grow up (I agree), but that doesn't change the fact that the quality of one's relationships affects the work that gets done.

Competency 1: Building Relationships

The first competency to assess in the area of social expertness is the candidate's ability to build and sustain good working relationships. Many positions require strong relationships across the enterprise; others may require strong relationships only within the person's immediate team. Still others require that a person be able to build strong relationships with people outside the organization. Many positions require people to be skilled at building relationships in all directions. According to Karl Albrecht in *Social Intelligence: The New Science of Success,* how you develop relationships with people makes them want to work with you, makes them want to work harder, and inspires them to be more committed to their work.[3] Consider the job of an executive headhunter. The headhunter must be able to build strong relationships with the hiring company. Then she must be able to build a trusting relationship with an executive who is successful and happy in his current position. Why would a successful and happy executive even talk to a headhunter? According to an article in *Personnel Today,* it's because of the headhunter's emotional intelligence skill of building a strong relationship with the potential candidate.[4]

Much research supports the value of building strong relationships at work.[5–8] Strong relationships at work, characterized by expressing caring, demonstrating support, sharing feelings and opinions, and deep listening, may even encourage resilience during times of change.[9] Employees' ability to build strong relationships also improves the overall climate within an organization. In addition, when strong relationships and social ties with coworkers are present, less turnover occurs.[10] Therefore, assessing a candidate's ability to build strong relationships can reap many benefits. As the interviewer or hiring manager, you will need to determine the necessary breadth of these relationships. As with many of the competencies of emotional intelligence, some job functions require the competency more than others.

Questions to Assess Building Relationships

Q: Who are some key people within your organization who you currently must work with on a regular basis to get your work done?
  - Describe your relationships with these people.

Q: Describe your present responsibility for building and maintaining relationships at work.
  - Whom do you build relationships with?
  - How?
  - Why?

Q: Tell me about a time when you were able to get something done at work because of a relationship you had with another person.

Q: Tell me about some of the people whom you have to work with on a regular basis that you find difficult to get along with.
  - What have you done to build stronger relationships with these people?

Q: Tell me about a situation when you "won someone over" at work.
  - What did you do?

Q: Tell me about someone who is resistant to you.
  - What did you do?

Q: Tell me about your relationship with your manager.
  - What works well?
  - What would you like to see improved?

Q: What do you do that makes you a good follower?

KEY POINTS TO CONSIDER WHEN ASSESSING ANSWERS

The interviewer should determine what steps the candidate takes to build relationships. Does she take active steps to build solid working relationships? Or is she unaware of how to build working relationships? Ideally, the candidate should recognize and take steps to actively build relationships. Evidence of steps would include being friendly toward others by saying good morning, asking if there is anything a coworker needs, inviting people to express concerns, listening to others' ideas, asking for input, following through on commitments, taking steps to include people in meetings, and finding ways to assist when possible. According to a study in the *Journal of Organizational Behavior Management,* these types of expressions of positive psychology in the workplace by peers and management lead to enhanced satisfaction, motivation, and productivity and create a positive workplace climate.[11] The proactive steps taken by the candidate should be work related. We're not looking for people who develop friendships at work. We're looking for candidates who value and take actions to build honorable and respectful working relationships.

When asking the candidate about someone who is difficult to get along with, look for evidence that the candidate has tried to build a relationship with the difficult coworker. A few people are just very contrary, and no amount of effort may change that. We don't expect candidates to have perfect working relationships with 100 percent of their coworkers, but we do expect candidates to get along well with most people. Be sure to probe if someone says he gets along with everyone. That's the kind of pat answer that begs for clarification. Respond with "It sounds like you're working with a great team. Most of us, however, at some point in our past, have encountered a team member that isn't easy to get along with. Can you tell me about someone in your past who was more difficult?"

Another important consideration is how the candidate views his relationship with his boss. Does he view the boss as someone with whom he should actively be taking steps to build a relationship? What is he doing to ensure a solid relationship? In this regard, the interviewer can assess how the candidate keeps his boss informed, how he supports his boss's mission, and how he works as a team member with his boss. The relationship with the boss is about being a good follower. What type of follower skills is the candidate expressing? Good followers are not yes-people. They are open to direction, offer suggestions, give honest input, put the department (and the boss) in the best light, seek to understand the department's mission, and help others within and outside the organization to get the best from their department.

Competency 2: Collaboration

In many projects and positions, collaboration is an essential job skill. Collaboration leads to improved solutions and employees' increased sense of ownership. Individual and organizational success and competitiveness today require collaboration because integration of ideas and information is critically important.[12] We define collaboration as the ability to invite others to share ideas by genuinely seeking input to problems or decisions. When people collaborate, they involve relevant stakeholders, build consensus, facilitate processes or systems, and record input.[13] Collaboration increases employees' ownership of ideas and level of commitment. A study in *Group and Organization Management* found that when workers were permitted to exercise personal control and to collaborate on solutions, they invested themselves more extensively and increased the psychological ownership of their work.[14] The hiring manager or interviewer must look for evidence that the candidate offers peers and others the opportunity to collaborate.

However, collaboration is a two-way street. Not only must a person invite others to offer ideas and solutions, but that same person must also be willing to offer his ideas and solutions to others. Sometimes people resist participating in workplace solutions. They prefer to keep their ideas private. These lone rangers do not see the value in collaboration. Still others use collaboration as a means to gain information and then take credit for the ideas of other people. These views not only damage the collaborative spirit in the workplace; they also decrease problem resolution and process improvement.

Consider these examples: Ben performed routine functions at the IT help desk. He found that users often called with the same problems. In the past, the help desk published responses to routine problems in an effort to reduce repetitive calls. Ben's affable nature allowed him to build relationships with several users across the network. Ben began to ask users whether they referred to the published responses before calling. As he investigated the situation, he learned that users did not find the published answers understandable. Ben began to rewrite the answers and asked users for input. After a year, repetitive calls were reduced by 27 percent. Ben's skills at collaboration engaged users and dramatically improved results for the department.

In another situation, Gary, the new shipping department supervisor, decided to reorganize supplies. He came in over the weekend, on his own time, and did a major reorganization of materials and supplies. He was eager to share the improvements with his staff on Monday morning. Instead, on Monday morning, his staff protested loudly. They felt completely left out of the decision to relocate supplies. In fact, most people had arranged the supplies to suit their own work habits. Not only did Gary not include his staff; he somehow managed to insult them. Although Gary's intentions and initiative were good, he demonstrated a failure to understand the value of collaboration.

Questions to Assess Collaboration

Q: Tell me how you recently solved a work problem.
- What process did you use?

Q: Describe a time when you had to solve a problem that involved or affected other people within the company.
- How did you solve it?

Q: Have you ever implemented an idea or solved a problem and had your solution meet with resistance?
- What do you think you could have done to avoid the resistance?

Q: Describe a time when you sought someone's ideas or opinions about a project or idea you were working on.

Q: Was there ever a time when you rejected someone's idea or opinion about a project?
- Tell me about that.

Q: Tell me about a time when you offered your idea or opinion to someone.

Q: Describe a time when your input improved someone's work.

Q: Have you ever offered an idea or opinion at work and had nothing to gain from it?
- Tell me about that.

KEY POINTS TO CONSIDER WHEN ASSESSING ANSWERS

The interviewer should be looking for two specific types of actions: actions that the candidate took to invite collaboration and actions that demonstrate that the candidate acted collaboratively with others.

The candidate should be able to describe times when he deliberately sought out the ideas or suggestions of others. As the interviewer or hiring manager, you should look for proactive steps on the part of the candidate that invite others into the problem-solving or idea phase of a project. Collaboration isn't about telling people afterward. That might qualify as good communication, but it's not collaboration. If collaboration is the competency that you desire, look for action steps. Also, follow up with questions that clarify the specific type of input the candidate was seeking. Also, ask follow-up questions to determine what the candidate did with the input. If the candidate asked for input but didn't use it, what steps did she take up front and afterward to ensure that people still felt respected or valued. Nothing can be more demoralizing than to be asked for input and then have that input ignored. Action steps to mitigate this type of situation might include asking for input on any of three acceptable solutions; telling people specific reasons why their input could not be used; and making clear to people that you are seeking advisers, not decision makers, in the process. However, a collaborative spirit goes beyond seeking advice. True collaboration requires that we sometimes surrender the decision making to the group process and that we facilitate a group process that will generate the best result. The interviewer will have to decide what approach is best suited to the job and the organization.

In addition, the candidate should be able to give examples of when she behaved in a collaborative manner to help others with their ideas or problems. The interviewer should listen for times when the candidate willingly offered ideas or solved problems without being asked. Also, the tone in which the candidate offers her ideas is very important. Is the candidate's tone helpful? Or is the candidate describing a time when she offered advice or input to someone in a way that might sound demeaning or arrogant? Here's an example: "I told Joe that the best way to do the job was to open the port before he started the process. I told him, but he didn't listen to me. It could have saved him a lot of time." This candidate offered her coworker some assistance, but it would be important to clarify exactly what transpired in this interchange. If you think the candidate may have communicated in a way that was arrogant or demeaning, be sure to ask for additional examples. If the candidate paints a consistent picture of offering ideas and having people reject them, you'd have to wonder if the rejection is inherent in the manner in which she is offering the ideas.

When asking questions about collaboration, look for a consistent behavior pattern that suggests that the candidate understands and values collaboration, and actively behaves in a way that promotes collaboration. The candidate who is truly collaborative is so because she believes in it, not because the organization expects her to be.

For some very senior people, collaboration may be seen as a competitive advantage, and the interviewer may be looking for evidence that senior people will have a vision that includes collaboration in the marketplace. Consider this comment by Paul Polman, CFO of Nestlé: "One of the core challenges of ECR [the retail industry's efficient consumer response] is to ensure that we foster collaboration when in so many areas we are competitors."[13]

Competency 3: Conflict Resolution

When people work together, conflict is inevitable. Conflict can stem from many different sources—a clash of ideas, personality, style, values, priorities, or just about anything else you can imagine. Our ability to resolve conflicts in our working relationships is critical. When people are skilled at conflict resolution, they are able to maintain a working relationship while openly discussing differences and coming to a resolution. Healthy conflict resolution allows coworkers to express differences in views for the purpose of learning and not for the purpose of demonstrating superiority over others. Therefore, conflict resolution involves dialogue because it enhances learning, according to Peter Senge.[16] It uncovers differences, but it also reveals commonality and helps to clarify and deepen understanding.

As you interview to determine how people resolve conflict, you must ask whether the candidate understands the value of dialogue in conflict resolution. Also, look for the methods that the candidate uses to resolve conflict. Does the person listen respectfully? Does she look for common ground? Does she try to understand the other person's point of view? Does she demonstrate empathy as she engages the other person? Does she openly ask what she could do to satisfy the conflict? Does she state her position clearly? Does the person use the most appropriate communication method for resolving conflict? For example, does the candidate attempt to resolve the conflict face-to-face, or through electronic means? E-mail communication is not the preferred way to resolve conflict because dialogue in this medium is difficult. Sometimes, if they are scattered throughout the United States or abroad, people have no choice in their method of communication, but generally, when the candidate talks about resolving a conflict with someone, try to determine whether she understands the value of talking face-to-face. In fact, one study noted that the potential for conflict is greater in teams whose members are distant and who rely on technology to communicate than in teams whose members can communicate in person.[17] This evidence strengthens the case for face-to-face communication in times of conflict.

Conflict resolution is an important skill for many different job functions, including leadership. The managers who perform best, as rated by both direct reports and their supervisors, score high in conflict resolution, according to a study released by the Tracom Group.[18] Leaders face conflicts over performance issues, policies, and procedures, and conflicts with peers. Interviewers and hiring managers should take special note of conflict-resolution skills if they are interviewing candidates for a leadership position. One manager, when asked about how he resolved a conflict with employees, said, "It's simple. I tell them if they don't like it here, they can leave." This approach doesn't leave much room for dialogue.

Q: Tell me about a dispute with a peer.
- What was it about?
- What did you do?
- How did it end up?

Q: Tell me about a time when someone suggested something that you disagreed with.
- What did you say?

Q: How have you resolved differences with peers or others?
- Tell me about the process you use to resolve your differences.

Q: Have you ever encountered someone at work who was unreasonable?
- What did you do?

For managers or leaders:

Q: Tell me about a time when there was a dispute between two coworkers.
- What did you do?

Q: Tell me about a time when you had a conflict with an employee.
- What did you do?
- How was it resolved?

Q: Describe a time when someone felt that you were unfair.
- What did you do?

Q: Relate an incident when someone verbally attacked you about something you said or did.
- What did you do?

KEY POINTS TO CONSIDER WHEN ASSESSING ANSWERS

Answering questions about conflict is uncomfortable for most candidates. Obviously, putting the candidate at ease is important. The interviewer should ask questions to gain a balanced view of the candidate's ability to address conflict. The interviewer will first want to assess whether the candidate typically avoids conflict or addresses the conflict head-on. This information will give the interviewer some indication of fit within a particular job. Most important, the interviewer will want to determine the candidate's skill level when addressing conflict. What steps or actions does the candidate take to resolve conflict? Does he look for common ground? Does he approach the conflict by putting his opponent at ease? If so, how does he do this? Does he assume the best and seek a win-win solution? What words does he use to accomplish this? You'll need to probe enough to gain a thorough understanding of the approach the candidate uses. An opening such as, "Juliana, I know that this is important to you, so I'd like to find a way for us to work together on this. I believe we can find a solution that will work for both of us," sets a win-win tone. It disarms the conflict. Another important consideration is whether the candidate openly states his concerns and needs and invites his opponent to do the same. The dialogue might sound like this: "Why don't you tell me what a positive resolution would look like, and I'll do the same for you. Maybe from there we can find some common ground." Again, the interviewer should be determining how the candidate engages in the conflict. Does it sound reasonable? Incredible as it may sound, when you ask people about a particular conflict, you will hear examples of how people take an extreme position or escalate the matter immediately by bringing it to a supervisor.

As the interviewer, you'll also receive information from the candidate regarding tolerance and diversity issues. People are not all the same, and sometimes personality or values are at the heart of the conflict. Is the candidate overly sensitive to people's differences? Does he require people to conform to his idea of what's right? These kinds of issues are quite important to assess. Sometimes, the skill that's needed is less one of conflict resolution and more one of understanding and valuing differences.

Another critical role is the one that a manager or supervisor takes when two people who report to her have a conflict. Does the candidate have a good track record of addressing these types of conflicts? What methods does she use? Is she building her staff's conflict-resolution skills in the process? Or is she rescuing her employees and constantly playing mediator? Also, is she bold enough to address conflicts that are interfering with teamwork, morale, and productivity?

One final thought on conflict resolution: Some people really are impossible to get along with. Most are not. If the candidate is placing many people in the category of "impossible," then perhaps it's the candidate who is impossible. Be sure to ask for multiple examples if you have any doubts.

Competency 4: Organizational Savvy

Skill and intellect are important attributes that a candidate needs to get the job done. However, skill and intellect will take a candidate only so far. Knowing how to get things done within an organization often requires people to have an understanding of the internal workings of the organization. By this we mean not just rules and regulations, but the savvy to gain sponsors for ideas and get people to buy in to one's proposals, a keen sense of timing, and an understanding of the who's who of decision making. What appears on a company's organizational chart and what happens in reality are often two different things.

Organizational savvy is defined as the ability to understand and maneuver within organizations to get things done. In certain jobs, the candidate's skill and savvy in organizational systems will play a vital role in his success. In a study of high-performing engineers at Bell Labs, Robert Kelley identified organizational savvy as one of the nine work strategies employed by star performers.[19] In an article in *Nature*, Deb Koen stated that mastery of technical skills accounts for only one-third of career success; the remaining two-thirds stems from organizational savvy.[20] Asking questions to gain insight into this area is very important for some positions. Generally, at the executive level, this skill is at least as critical to success as a person's technical ability.

In one example, Tammy demonstrated organizational savvy as she advanced an idea to spend more on research and development. Tammy constructed a well-developed plan, but she knew that it would take more than a plan to convince the board to increase spending at the pace she suggested. She knew that one of the directors would favor her plan. She also knew that two others would oppose it. However, Tammy knew that the director who favored her plan and the two that opposed it resisted one another. So, rather than select the director who favored her plan to sponsor it, she decided to approach the remaining neutral members one by one. Her approach worked.

Questions to Assess Organizational Savvy

Q: Did you ever have an opportunity to advance a new idea at your last job?
   - How did you go about doing that?

Q: Tell me about a time when you gained support for an idea that you had.
   - How did you do that?
   - Why was this idea important to you?

Q: Describe a time when you couldn't get support for an idea that you had.
   - What happened?
   - Why was this idea important to you?

Q: Within your present position, what happens when you run into someone who isn't supporting your efforts to get things done?
   - Describe what you do.

Q: Have you ever had someone undermine your efforts?
   - What did you do?

Q: How can you tell who makes decisions in your organization?

Q: Tell me about a time when you needed support from peers in order to get an idea across.
   - How did you gain that support?
   - Why was it important to you to get that particular idea or initiative accomplished?

KEY POINTS TO CONSIDER WHEN ASSESSING ANSWERS

As an interviewer or hiring manager, if you've made the decision that organizational savvy is important to getting certain jobs done, you'll have to assess whether or not the candidate will fit in and understand your organization and have the skills to grasp the dynamics that lead to success. From the candidate's responses to the questions listed above, you should be able to determine whether he has an understanding that how he approaches people, and whom he approaches, is part of an overall strategy to gain support. The candidate should be able to articulate why certain individuals are key and what methods or tactics he used to gain an individual's support. Also, the candidate should be able to recognize that each idea is different and may require a different approach to move it forward. You should be able to determine whether the candidate understands and exerts energy to build a strategy to get things done. One candidate said, "I don't think about how to get ideas across; I just put them out there and see what happens."

Next, focus on whether the candidate has the kinds of relationships that extend across the organization and whether the candidate knows how to engender other people's support. Look for genuine relationships and support with a wide range of people who are willing to help the candidate. These relationships should not be based solely on an attitude of "I'll support you if you support me." The relationships should be more genuine and should be based on trust and respect. The way the candidate describes the support and how he gains sponsors is often very telling. One candidate actually said, "I told Henry that if he expects support for his next initiative, he'd better support me on this." This kind of ultimatum is not the way to create true teamwork.

The candidate will need the ability to read the climate within an organization or even within a meeting in order to be able to assess timing, opportunity, and key players. What is the candidate telling you about her assessment of climate and culture? One candidate, when asked about bringing ideas to fruition, said that every week at the senior staff meeting, there was time on the agenda for each senior staff member to discuss enterprisewide improvement ideas. She said that the tone in some of those meetings was rushed or negative. She noticed that when the meeting tone was rushed, the plant manager often killed ideas with quick one-liners such as "It's a good idea, but I don't think we have time for that kind of initiative." She also noticed that if the production meeting preceding the staff meeting was negative, then rather than entertain new ideas for improvement, the plant manager would say, "We need to focus on getting our numbers up." The candidate said she realized that these two situations were simply not conducive to the climate needed to "sell" an idea or initiative. She acknowledged that while the plant manager was very powerful, he was also very open and reasonable, as long as he was approached at the right time. This candidate's responses to the interviewer's questions indicated that she was able to give specific examples that supported her position. It was obvious that she had the ability to read important information about the climate in her previous position, which allowed her to advance her ideas.

Understanding the candidate's motives or intentions also proves valuable. Is the candidate advancing goals that are for the good of the organization or is he simply building himself up? You should listen for intention. Although it may be difficult to determine intention, by asking questions about why the candidate was pursuing particular ideas, you'll gain a sense of what the candidate values. One candidate talked about several ideas that he was trying to advance at directors' meetings. These ideas could be grouped under the heading "gaining a larger piece of the organization under his control." Now, it's not unreasonable to want to gain control of things that impact your operation, but the interviewer began to wonder whether this was the best plan for the organization. As the interviewer pressed and asked follow-up questions about why these ideas were worth pursuing, she uncovered the candidate's motive, expressed in his own words: "I knew if I could get all of these pieces of the organization under my umbrella, then the board would have little choice but to make me the next executive VP." That motivation is not necessarily bad, but it does require that the interviewer or hiring manager take a second look.

FIGURE 6.1 Social Expertness at a Glance

	PRO	CONS
Building Relationships	• Gives concrete examples of positive steps taken to develop work relationships • Can identify and call people as resources because of relationships he has established • Demonstrates sincere valuing of others • Demonstrates actions to build relationships with difficult people • Offers support to others for ideas, projects, etc.	• Lacks examples of specific behaviors taken to build relationships • Is unable to recognize need to develop relationships with others • Dismisses difficult people • Initially responds by circumventing difficult people • Keeps score in relationships as evidenced by "He owes me."
Collaboration	• Gives concrete examples of involving others • Discusses value of input from others in specific situations • Gives examples of offering input to others • Doesn't wait until project is complete before involving others	• Is unable to give concrete examples of seeking input from others • Is unable to give examples of offering input to others • Emphasizes mostly role of self versus contribution of others • Sees others' input as criticism
Conflict Resolution	• Is able to give examples of viable solutions to conflict • Is able to articulate the conflict in unbiased terms • Demonstrates conflict resolution actions such as listening, open discussion, and dialogue • Discusses conflict in terms of what was learned, not what was gained • Values conflict resolution over avoidance • Recognizes that conflict resolution produces better results	• Frames conflict as a win-lose • Devalues the other person when describing the conflict • Emphasizes the conflict's impact on self with little or no acknowledgment of impact on others • Discusses the conflict in terms of what was gained • Avoids conflict at all costs • Placates others to avoid conflict • Comprises own values to avoid conflict

FIGURE 6.1 *Continued*

	PRO	CONS
Organizational Savvy	• Gives concrete, realistic examples of advancing ideas • Gives evidence of recognizing decision-making processes and alignments within the organization • Gives examples of using organizational savvy to organization's best interest • Uses unwritten rules to achieve what's best for the organization	• Is unable to give examples of how to advance ideas or suggestions • Uses knowledge of organization to advance own cause or position • Is unable to describe the organization's decision-making channels • Either undervalues or overvalues the "unwritten rules" within organizations

Endnotes

1. Robert E. Kelley, *How to Be a Star at Work* (New York: Times Business, Random House, 1998).
2. Craig Chappelow and Jean Britton Leslie, "Keeping Your Career on Track," *Center for Creative Leadership News* 20,6 (2001): 6.3.
3. Karl Albrecht, Social Intelligence: *The New Science of Success* (San Francisco: Josey-Bass, 2006).
4. V. Matthews, "View from the Top," *Personnel Today* (Spring 2007): 19.
5. W.H. Bergquist, *The Postmodern Organization: Mastering the Art of Irreversible Change* (San Francisco: Jossey-Bass, 1993); Bridges 1991; Fletcher 2001; Wheatly 2002.
6. W. Bridges, *Managing Transitions: Making the most of change* (New York: Addison Wesley, 1991).
7. J. Fletcher, *Disappearing Acts: Gender, Power, and Relational Practice at Work* (Cambridge: MIT Press, 2001).
8. M. J. Wheatley, *Turning to One Another: Simple Conversations to Restore Hope to the Future* (San Francisco: Berrett-Koehler, 2002).
9. Sandra M. Wilson and Shann R. Ferch, "Enhancing Resilience in the Workplace Through the Practice of Caring Relationships," *Organization Development Journal* (Winter 2005): 45.
10. Amy E. Randle and Annette Ranft, "Motivations to Maintain Social Ties with Coworkers: The Moderating Role of Turnover Intentions on Information Exchange," *Group and Organizational Management* 32, 2 (April 2007): 208.

11. Andrew J. Martin, "The Role of Positive Psychology in Enhancing Satisfaction, Motivation, and Productivity in the Workplace," *Journal of Organizational Behavior Management* 24, 1–2 (2004–5): 113.
12. Dee Dickinson, "Lifelong Learning for Business: A Global Perspective" (presented at the Conference on Lifelong Learning for European Business, Oxford University, UK, October 6–7, 1992).
13. Rees Morrison, "How to Make Collaboration Work: Powerful Ways to Build Consensus, Solve Problems, and Make Decisions," *Consulting to Management* (September 2004): 62.
14. Michael P. O'Driscoll, Jon L. Pierce, and Ann-Marie Coghlan, "The Psychology of Ownership: Work Environment Structure, Organizational Commitment, and Citizenship Behaviors," *Group and Organization Management* 31, 3 (June 2006): 388.
15. Paul Polman, "Learning from Long Experience," *ECR Journal: International Commerce Review* 6, 1 (Spring 2006): 70.
16. Peter Senge, *The Fifth Discipline* (New York: Doubleday Currency, 2006).
17. Pamela J. Hinds and Diane E. Bailey, "Out of Sight, Out of Sync: Understanding Conflict in Distributed Teams," *Organizational Science* 14, 6 (November–December 2003): 615.
18. "New Research Proves Interpersonal Skills Make High-Performing Managers; Study Shows That Building Effective Relationships Is Critical to Managerial Success," *Business Wire,* August 31, 2005, 1.
19. Kelley, *How to Be a Star at Work.*
20. Deb Koen, "Naturejobs Career View," *Nature,* May 5, 2005, 126.

CHAPTER 7

Personal Influence:
Influencing Self

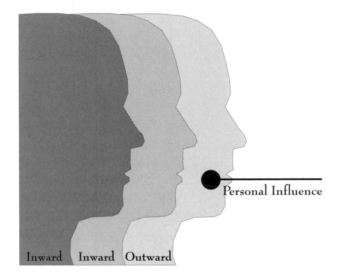

Inward Inward Outward

Personal Influence

Competency 1—Self-Confidence
Competency 2—Initiative and Accountability
Competency 3—Goal Orientation
Competency 4—Optimism
Competency 5—Flexibility and Adaptability

Personal influence is defined as one's ability to positively lead and inspire others as well as oneself. In this chapter we address influencing self; in Chapter 8, we address influencing others.

So often, the qualities that separate the accomplished from those who eke by relate to the internal register that drives people. Talent and brilliance waste away when housed in a self that lacks confidence, initiative, goals, and a positive outlook. Success in nearly all forms comes down to self. The actions that we take and the attitude that surrounds them define where we go in life. If we can't influence ourselves, victory eludes us. In fact, if we can't influence ourselves, not only does victory elude us, but we don't even play the game. The interview process must consider the qualities and competencies that drive the self to high performance. Those qualities include the following competencies:

1. *Self-confidence,* which is appropriately believing in one's skills or abilities;

2. *Initiative and accountability,* which is being internally guided to take steps or actions and taking responsibility for those actions;

3. *Goal orientation,* which is setting goals for oneself and living and working toward those goals;

4. *Optimism,* which is having a tendency to look at the bright side of things and to be hopeful for the best; and

5. *Flexibility and adaptability,* which is the ability to adapt to the needs of others or situations as appropriate.

Competency 1: Self-Confidence

People who have realistic confidence in their abilities and who portray those abilities to others are said to be self-confident. Being self-confident means you are far more likely to aspire to great things, take risks, overcome challenges, grow, and succeed.[1] Self-confidence helps us to take on difficult tasks. It enables us to lead, influence, and persuade others. "People look to leaders to show confidence in the direction they are taking—it's motivating," says Richard Doyle, director of group organizational effectiveness at Cadbury Schweppes.[2]

Self-confidence is embedded in the subtle manners and behaviors that a person portrays. It is embedded in the language and words a person chooses and even in the body language that a person displays. But mostly, it is an internal perception that a person carries of his abilities and skills. As a hiring manager or interviewer, you'll have the entire interview process to look for evidence of a person's display of confidence. You will want to determine, however, whether the display of confidence is based on realistic results.

Depending on the position, a person's ability to display confidence may be very highly regarded. Of course, there's always that fine line between confidence and arrogance. The interview process can help you distinguish between the two. The confident candidate clearly takes a position yet somehow leaves room for exchange and discourse. During the exchange or discourse, a confident person will listen carefully, not to discredit, but to really test his case and consider new information. The arrogant candidate clearly tells you who is right and dismisses any exchange or discourse on the subject. If an exchange or discourse does take place, an arrogant person somehow indicates that by your asking a question or presenting another view, you show that you don't quite comprehend the issue.

Consider these situations: Carol is a director at a large multinational company. She builds strong relationships with her peers and the executives within the company. When she speaks to executives, she states her case in clear language. She speaks directly to people and she speaks directly to the issues. She doesn't apologize for her opinions; she simply states them. She doesn't put qualifiers in her statements. She states facts and quickly lets people know how she's come to her conclusions. When she talks, people listen. Yet she's open to discussion and welcomes others' viewpoints. She listens carefully and tries to find the holes in her own case. Because she is confident, convincing, and open, people often adopt her positions, or, at a minimum, she gets the discussions started to effect needed change.

In our second example, Tom is also a director at a large company. Contrary to Carol's, his manner is wishy-washy and leaves people wondering about his opinions and positions. Qualifiers fill his language. He quickly retreats if someone challenges something that he says. A typical statement from Tom sounds like this: "Although I'm not really sure, maybe it wouldn't hurt if we might try . . ." Most executives aren't looking for "maybes" or "mights." For goodness' sake, Tom, take a stand.

Questions to Assess Self-Confidence

Q: Tell me about a time when you took on a task that you considered "out of your comfort zone."
- How did you feel?
- Why did you do it?
- Did you think you were going to succeed or fail?

Q: If you were going to try to persuade me regarding something, how would you do it?

Q: Describe a time when you interjected a different point of view or a different side of an issue.
- How did you go about doing that?

Q: Tell me about a time when you were confident enough to disagree with something or someone.

Q: Tell me about your strengths.
- How do you know they are your strengths?
- How do you measure your strengths?
- What feedback have you gotten that indicates that this quality is a strength?

Q: Tell me about a time that you were concerned about being successful at a task or you thought you were going to fail.
- What did you do?

Q: When do you typically ask for assistance?
- Describe the last time you asked for help on something.

Q: How do you think you're going to perform at this job?

For managers and leaders:

Q: Tell me about a time when you had to implement a change.
- What did you say to your staff?
- How did you convince them to follow you?

Q: Tell me about a time when you had to lead others in a certain direction and you had some doubts.
- What did you do?
- What did you say?

Q: Have you ever experienced a time when others questioned your ability to lead?
- Tell me about that.
- What did you do?

KEY POINTS TO CONSIDER WHEN ASSESSING ANSWERS

The entire interview process is useful for assessing a candidate's confidence level. How does the candidate project his ideas and answers? Is the candidate willing to take a stand? Or is the candidate quick to retract his comments? What level of commitment does the candidate have to his answers? What are the candidate's nonverbal characteristics communicating? Confident people stand up straight, smile more than less confident people, and make eye contact.[3] Throughout the interview process, you will be able to assess the level of confidence the candidate projects.

Balancing the candidate's presentation with facts is also quite useful. After all, you want to make sure that the candidate's confidence is based in reality. Asking questions about strengths and following up with questions to determine how the person knows his strengths is often worthwhile. Listen for statements that provide evidence, such as "Every year it appears on my performance appraisal"; "Every boss I have tells me that time management is one of my strengths"; "My teammates rely on me for my organizational skills"; "I have achieved results such as——by using this strength." Remember, sometimes a candidate needs to be encouraged to talk about his strengths. Even someone who is confident in his abilities may not always be comfortable telling others about it because it may feel boastful. Encourage the candidate to tell you about areas where he really feels confident. Don't confuse humility for lack of self-confidence. A person can be very confident about a skill or ability, yet feel as though it is inappropriate to tell others about it.

It also takes confidence to voice ideas and opinions. Look for evidence from the candidate about when she voiced her ideas or opinions. Ask how she went about it. You'll also get a clear picture of a person's confidence by asking questions that allow the candidate to describe situations when she voiced a contrary point of view and the manner in which she communicated it.

To determine confidence versus arrogance, try to challenge the candidate on something. Does she become argumentative? Or is she interested in learning more about your position? Also, look for subtle body language. One candidate subtly shook her head in a quick dismissive manner when the interviewer presented an opposing viewpoint. Appropriately confident people listen to others, think about the issues, and have a more holistic view of life than those who are arrogant. People who are realistically self-confident make a balanced assessment.[4]

People who are confident also are willing to admit that they need assistance. Has the candidate ever asked for help? A project can be jeopardized if someone involved doesn't have the skill or information to complete the job, but it can be more of a crisis if that person lacks the confidence to speak up. Therefore, it's useful to ask a client how he typically knows when to ask for assistance. This line of questioning is also helpful to determine whether someone lacks confidence to try a few solutions on his own. Is the candidate willing to act independently or must he always stop and ask for direction? Confidence could be a key factor in this person's success.

But what if all indications suggest that the candidate is self-confident? Could there still be cause for concern? Yes. Overconfidence is the hallmark of a narcissist. Asking a candidate, "How do you think you're going to perform on this job?" poses a purely hypothetical question. It is not a behavior-based question. Evidence suggests that narcissists generally predict future performance based on expectation, not actual performance.[5] If a person unequivocally states that she would do a great job and does not back that proclamation with facts about past performance, it may be cause for concern. Chapter 10 contains more information to help the interviewer make a balanced judgment.

COMPETENCY 2: INITIATIVE AND ACCOUNTABILITY

Initiative drives action. In other words, this intrinsic quality motivates a person to act. Although action alone does not lead to accomplishment or performance, lack of action certainly thwarts accomplishment or performance. This self-directed force presents itself in all high performers. Of course, initiative coupled with skill or talent delivers the highest-quality results. Competitive business must rely on employees' initiatives to seek out opportunities and respond to customers' needs.[6] Managers simply cannot be aware of all the opportunities and customer needs that an employee encounters each day. They cannot hover over employees all day, directing them. (Besides, that behavior would likely kill any independent action the employee might have taken.) Actions must come from the employee's internal drive.

High performers take the initiative and also take accountability for their actions. Accountability suggests that we accept the consequences of our actions. First we take the action, and then we stand behind the action by taking responsibility for it. We couple these attributes because initiative without accountability can lead to negative behaviors. For example, we may have encountered a person who takes the initiative to do something, but then places blame on others if it doesn't work out. Of course, leadership plays an important role in creating a climate where both initiative and accountability are rewarded.

Consider the following examples. Charlene is a highly educated research scientist. She is a member of a special group of researchers who are working together to determine the cause of various immune disorders. She and her fellow researchers meet weekly to discuss possible theories; then each scientist works alone to examine the possibilities within the theories. Each week, the researchers are excited to come together to discuss their findings. However, each week, Charlene has excuse after excuse about her (lack of) work. She finds reasons to put things off, makes excuses, finds fault, or argues the direction of the team. One of her colleagues, frustrated with her behavior, said, "You know, the problem is that you are just lazy and aren't willing to do the hard work that this position requires." It's hard to determine the true nature of the problem with Charlene, but one thing is certain: work requires just that—work. If we lack the initiative to put the effort into something, the results are going to suffer.

Another, subtler, example involves Carl. Carl is full of good ideas. He has ideas about everything—how to improve the organization's processes, suppliers, customer interaction, policies, and so on. However, Carl doesn't ever do anything to advance these ideas. Just once, it would be interesting to see Carl take action to advance an idea. He's been labeled a chronic complainer. Yet, if you look within his comments and complaints, he really does have some solid ideas. If he had taken the initiative to change some of the things he complains about, his complainer label would likely change to superhero.

Questions to Assess Initiative and Accountability

Q: Tell me about a time when you decided on your own that something needed to be done.
- What did you do?

Q: Describe a time when you did more than was required on your job.
- How did you feel about that?

Q: Have you ever made any improvements to your work without being asked?
- Give me some examples.
- How did you do it?

Q: When you perform your present job, have you ever thought about a way to improve the quality of the product or service that you provide?
- Tell me about that.

Q: Have you ever come up with a way to cut costs in your present position?
- What did that entail?
- How did you go about doing it?

Q: Have you ever thought of a way to perform your present job in less time?

What did you do about it?

Q: Tell me about a time when something you did resulted in a change for your department or area.

How did you go about doing it?

How did you feel about that?

Q: Have you ever taken the initiative to do something that didn't work out?

Describe that situation.

What did you do?

How did you feel about that?

Q: Have you ever solved a work-related problem that had been a problem for a long time?

What did you do?

How did you do it?

Q: Have you ever taken an action and gotten blamed when it didn't work out?

Describe what happened.

KEY POINTS TO CONSIDER WHEN ASSESSING ANSWERS

Initiative is a key factor desirable in many job functions. Interviewers or hiring managers will want to screen candidates to determine whether they act on their own initiative. Candidates should cite examples of actions they have taken to improve quality, cost, timeliness, or customer service. The key word here is "actions." Having a great idea is one thing, but how did the candidate act on her idea? Did the candidate act independently to improve things that were within her control? Otherwise, did the candidate engage others to advance an idea that was for the good of the department or team? How? Did she just tell the boss and let the boss deal with it, or was she a dynamic partner in taking action to change something? Of course, the interviewer or hiring manager will need to evaluate the scope of independent action the candidate was able to exercise. For example, in some companies, it would not be possible for a frontline employee to change a procedure independently. But don't underestimate the actions that a determined person without positional power could take to influence changes. The interviewer should be evaluating *whether* the person takes actions, as well as *how* the person takes actions. Both features are important. A person who organizes a union is demonstrating initiative. But it may not be in the best interest or fit for the hiring company. The interviewer should be certain to ask "how" questions to determine what form the candidate's initiative takes.

Also important to keep in mind when asking a candidate about initiative is to ask how the candidate felt about the situation. Sometimes people take initiative, but then feel resentful that they had to perform the burden of the work. A question such as "Describe a time when you did more than was required on your job. How did you feel about that?" allows the interviewer to determine the candidate's feelings about going above and beyond. Sometimes candidates will take the initiative, but they will not do so because of a service orientation. Asking about the candidate's feelings will give the interviewer a new dimension of information. Some people take initiative and then play the hero. Still others play the martyr. Both of these roles can be destructive in the workplace.

Similarly, determining how the candidate reacts when he has taken initiative and it doesn't work out gives the interviewer important data. Does the candidate stop trying? Does he regroup and find another strategy? Or does he decide on another initiative as the focus for his energy? All of these details will give the interviewer useful insight. When asked about an initiative that didn't work out, one candidate said, "I figured, I wasn't going to waste my time and energy, so I decided to leave." With some probing, the interviewer discovered that this was a pattern of behavior that the candidate had displayed with a string of other employers. Some employees place blame if their actions don't work out. Here again, probing offers insight into how employees respond to initiatives that don't work out.

Competency 3: Goal Orientation

Does the candidate have clear goals in mind? Is the candidate driven by internal and external goals? Is the candidate able to set goals for himself? Setting and working toward goals distinguishes high-performing candidates. Goal orientation is different from initiative. Initiative is about taking action; goal orientation sets the direction for the action. Someone can take initiative but not necessarily be clearly focused in terms of direction or goals. If a job demands setting and achieving goals, considering a person's internal mechanism for goal orientation leads the interviewer to some fruitful information. Many companies' performance-management systems require candidates to set goals. Goal setting is hardly a new science for most people. However, these questions concern the candidate's internal goal-setting drive, not a company-driven process.

In management and leadership positions, an individual's goal orientation must be extended to setting goals for others. When setting up a team, the manager must make the goals clear to all members.[7] However, according to a survey by Hay Group, a key reason people leave organizations is because they believe their companies lack direction; only 27 percent said their organizations have a clear sense of direction. Therefore, when assessing managers and leaders, you are looking for not only individual goal orientation, but also the candidate's ability to set goals with others and to give others a clear sense of direction.

Consider these examples. Hector is the top salesman in a national drug company. When asked about how he continues his performance year after year, Hector quickly stated, "It's all about setting goals. You won't perform unless you have clear goals that you are working toward. Every day I create a goal of so many contacts. I don't give up until I've met my goal. Period." There is no doubt that Hector is also highly skilled in his craft, but many highly skilled people do not achieve great results. Hector's ability to set goals and stick to them clearly sets him apart.

Another example of successful goal orientation comes from James. James is a counselor at a state penitentiary. This can be a difficult and draining profession because of the rate of recidivism. James meets the mandatory goals and measures such as client contact hours, number of clients, mandatory drug tests, and so on. However, in addition, James decided that he wanted to institute his own types of goals to keep himself motivated. He decided that for each client, he would establish some type of breakthrough behavior as the goal. For example, a breakthrough behavior might be when an inmate decides to voluntarily join a help group or read a book. James works with each inmate to help the inmate achieve the breakthrough behavior. Each time, James says it keeps him motivated and it also helps to put the inmate on a path to success.

Questions to Assess Goal Orientation

Q: Describe some goals for your present position.
- How were these goals determined?
- Do you meet these goals on a regular basis?

Q: Have you ever thought that these goals were unrealistic?
- Why?

Q: Have you ever had a goal at work that you didn't meet?
- How did you feel about that?

Q: Tell me about a goal that you imposed on yourself at work.
- Why did you decide on that particular goal?

Q: Tell me about a time when you didn't achieve something that you set out to do.
- What happened?
- How did you feel about that?

Q: What goals do you have right now?

Q: What goals did you accomplish last year?

Q: Tell me about a time when you didn't feel like working.
- What did you do?

Q: Describe your process for setting goals for yourself.

For the manager or leader:

Q: How do you set goals for those who report to you?

- Describe the process you use to set goals within your unit or department.

Q: How have you helped others set goals?

Q: How do you ensure that the goals are aligned with the business strategy?

Q: Tell me about a time when someone who reported to you did not reach an important goal.
  - What did you do?

KEY POINTS TO CONSIDER WHEN ASSESSING ANSWERS

When evaluating goal orientation, keep in mind the position and the types of goals required. Some positions may require short-term goals —goals that can be achieved within the day or even within the hour. Setting goals can be as simple as writing five things to do on a piece of paper and deciding to get them done before lunch. Other positions will require the candidate to set long-term goals. In both cases, the interviewer should be listening for specific, clear goals set by the individual.

To begin the discussion on goals, you can ask about the goals the candidate must achieve in order to successfully complete her work. Each job should have goals, and the candidate should recognize what those goals are. (If the candidate is working in a situation that does not have recognized or stated goals, then don't punish the candidate for a poor work situation. Instead, shift the focus to what goals she has set for herself.) The initial discussion about goals in her present position will help the candidate focus on goals at work. Also, you'll gain insight into the candidate's opinions about working toward goals. Does she consider goals an imposition? Or does she consider them helpful?

Next, shift the discussion to self-imposed goals, and seek evidence of them in the candidate. Look for times when the candidate decided on and met these goals at work. Although self-imposed goals related to outside activities (golf scores, exercise, dieting) are useful to determine if the candidate has the ability to set goals and follow though, it's important to determine whether the candidate considers the workplace a place where self-imposed goal setting is of value. After all, your purpose is to evaluate whether the person will set goals at work, not in her personal life.

You'll also want to determine whether the person is capable of reaching goals. Some people are great at setting goals, but reaching them is another thing. Evaluate the results the candidate achieved.

Lastly, you'll want to consider how the candidate reacts when she doesn't meet a goal—imposed by either others or herself. Does she rationalize? Blame others? Give up in defeat? What happens to the candidate's motivation in these instances?

If you're interviewing a manager, you'll want to know about her goal setting as well as her ability to help others set and reach goals. Does she impose goals on others? Does she see goal setting as a collaborative effort? What technique does she apply if goals aren't reached? How does she help others achieve their goals? Most people respond best to a collaborative goal-setting process. Also, does the leader see herself as a partner and resource for assisting people in reaching their goals?

Competency 4: Optimism

In *Learned Optimism,* author Martin Seligman said that optimism is associated with many desirable outcomes, including positive mood and good morale, perseverance and effective problem solving, occupational success, popularity, good health, and even long life and freedom from trauma.[8] Therefore, in many positions, a candidate's view of the world affects his ability to maneuver and gain success within his world. If a candidate views the world as overwhelming and negative, he may lack the energy or willingness to take on difficult tasks. This worldview affects performance as well as the attitudes of coworkers and others in the workplace.[9] Therefore, depending on the position, the interviewer's inquiry into a candidate's optimism can prove telling. Does the candidate display positive energy and enthusiasm, or is the candidate filled with doom and gloom? Is the candidate willing to take risks and try new methods or procedures because he's hopeful that he may find a better way, or is he paralyzed by the "it will never work" philosophy? Is he apt to give up when he's down by ten runs in the last inning, or does he remain hopeful and give his best to the

 THE EQ INTERVIEW

last pitch? Research indicates that the best hires are the people who are likable in terms of attitude and optimism.[10]

Consider the following examples. The successful salesperson is the classic example of optimism in motion. If the salesperson constantly thought that the next prospect was going to reject his proposal, it wouldn't take long for him to give up and find a new profession. Actually, he wouldn't have to give up, because his performance would force the issue. One very successful salesperson said that he always believes that the next person he talks to will be "the big one." If it turns out that he doesn't make the sale, then he convinces himself that he's one more rejection closer to "the big one." Therefore, he thinks about every person, both before and after the encounter, as helping him reach his goals. How's that for optimism at work?

A less obvious example is provided by a call-center operator who is plagued all day by calls from customers who are having problems and who are often angry or upset. This optimistic operator says that she believes that in nearly every call, she is able to help the caller gain a resolution to the problem. She says that she focuses on what she can do to help and says that this conveys to customers that she is on their side.

Another example, one that plays out in the IT department of a large financial institution, also demonstrates that the way one thinks about the work affects the work. One programmer gets so pessimistic about reaching the programming deadlines that the whole team begins to feel stressed. A teammate described it like this: "We'll be humming along on a project and then Joe will start with his predictions . . . 'We'll be lucky if we get to phase two in six months rather than three months. Harry is already behind on his portion of the project; it will be impossible for us to get things done without Harry's piece. Sue isn't going to get the testing done. She's always late.'" This kind of pessimism saps people's energy.

Questions to Assess Optimism

Q: Tell me about a project that you knew was not going to deliver results.

• How did you know?

Q: Describe a time when you tried something new at work. How did that work?

- Would you do it again?
- Why or why not?

Q: Describe a situation at work when you were optimistic and it affected the outcome.

Q: Describe a situation at work when others wanted to move forward on something and you didn't think it was a good idea.

- Why didn't you think it would work?
- What did you do?

Q: Describe a time when you were more optimistic than others at work about a particular project.

- What did you do?

Q: Tell me about a time when you had misplaced optimism.

- How did you proceed?

Q: Tell me about a time when you didn't believe that a project was going to turn out on time, on budget, or on track.

- Why did you think it was going to be a problem?

Q: Give me a situation where you believed that something was going to be successful and it was.

- How did you know?

Q: Tell me about a time when someone on your team was negative about an outcome.

- How did it affect you?

KEY POINTS TO CONSIDER WHEN ASSESSING ANSWERS

Optimism isn't intended to compensate for poor project planning, poor sales skills, or poor customer service. When you're evaluating the candidate's answers to the above questions, you're going to have to take into consideration and balance the data the candidate is giving you against the attitude the candidate has about the situation. If the data clearly suggest that poor skills or poor planning is an issue, the candidate's optimism won't make a difference. However, the spirit of these questions is to try to determine what perspective the candidate brings to the team. Listen for positive statements and a hopeful perspective that the candidate brings when describing past situations. Find out about the candidate's tolerance for others who are optimistic. Does the candidate have a positive regard for hopefulness or optimism, or does he view such thinking with contempt? Sure, facts and data are important, and certain candidates trained in certain disciplines will rely more than others on facts, but often underlying the facts is a person's belief about a particular situation. In this situation, you'll be listening for the underlying belief.

Also, listen for how the candidate describes the causes of bad events. Those who explain bad events in a circumscribed way, with external, unstable, and specific causes, are described as optimistic. In the learned-helplessness model, people become helpless. This learned helplessness is represented as a generalized expectation that future outcomes will be unrelated to actions.[11] Therefore, a candidate will sound like a victim—he will express that no matter what he had done, the outcome wouldn't have improved. The victim voice says that "nothing is my fault."[12] Listen for this type of victim voice from the candidate.

Here's an example of what one candidate said when asked about a project that she didn't think would work: "I just saw this as one more project that wouldn't produce the result that management promised. I just get tired of their pie-in-the-sky promises." Although the candidate may be right about management's thinking, further probing is in order. When the interviewer asked for an example of projects that didn't produce a result as promised, the candidate said after some hesitation, "Well, they said that a program fix would eliminate errors by 17 percent. It didn't." Further probing about the results revealed the following: "It only produced a 15 percent improvement in errors." Maybe management was a bit optimistic, but it seems like the results speak for themselves.

Competency 5: Flexibility and Adaptability

Change is routine in most workplaces. Rapid change is the norm in many. Without flexibility, we render ourselves victims of the constant change that defines life. Our ability to meet the world where it stands today and where it heads tomorrow depends largely on our ability to be flexible or to adapt. Flexibility in our thinking, flexibility in our decision making, and flexibility in our behavior enable us to respond to ever-changing conditions, situations, people.

Flexibility demands that we sometimes let go of the past so that we can prepare for the future. Are we able to see what's on the horizon and adjust accordingly, or do we rigidly adhere to doing things the way they've been done in the past? Adapting to technology, new markets, global influences, mergers and acquisitions, new systems, new bosses, new building space, and even virtual space all exercise our flexibility muscle. One thing is certain: the rate of change will continue and accelerate. Change in organizations today is frequent and fast paced, creating what Bergquist calls a liquid state of existence characterized by "edges of shifting boundaries" and a turbulence that creates a sense of chaos and confusion.[13]

This competency is largely associated with change, but it also applies to the way we interact with others. For example, do we bend to other's needs, or do we rigidly follow only our own demands? Are we able to rearrange our schedules to accommodate others, or must we maintain the timetable conceived in our minds? Do we engender a sense of meeting people on their terms? Or do we demand that everyone play on our turf? Give-and-take defines these flexible interactions with others. We're not suggesting that people compromise important values; instead, we're looking for candidates who know when to hold their ground and know when it doesn't matter.

Another critical factor is to know when to let go of successful behaviors. At first blush, that statement may sound absurd. Why would you want or need to let go of behaviors that garnered you success? Because the behaviors that earned you success in one position or with one set of people and experiences may cause failure with another set of people or in another experience. Emotional intelligence demands that we use the ability to read the environment and then adjust our behavior to obtain the desired result. One example is the frontline manager who gets promoted to a higher-level position. Maybe part of that frontline manager's success rested on her ability to manage the small details. At a higher level of leadership, this may be the trait that causes failure. If she relates to peers by attempting to micromanage them, she may fail to gain their respect or cooperation. Another common example is the technical expert who is promoted to supervisor and must let go of jumping in and solving problems and instead revert to a coaching role to assist others in solving problems. These people must let go of the very behaviors that created their success. But more important, they must have the awareness to understand that these behaviors will no longer produce the result they require in their new roles. Then they must be flexible by behaving in a manner suitable to their new positions.

Consider these examples in the workplace. Connie's twenty years of experience make her an ideal person to assist in developing a new system that will streamline the process of adjustments in the financial institution where she works. But Connie is stuck. She focuses on the past. She is unable or unwilling to take her experience and think about how the new technology can be helpful. Her lack of flexibility causes her to complain and resist change. Instead of being helpful, her experience proves to be a hindrance.

In another example, Kiel is the first to volunteer in a small business. If you have a job that needs to be done, you can count on Kiel to take it on. Need someone to work on a customer complaint? No problem; Kiel will do it. Need someone to test a new process? No problem; Kiel will do it. Need someone to drive the owner to the airport? No problem; Kiel will do it. That kind of flexibility is very refreshing. But it's also good for Kiel. He's constantly learning new things, meeting new people, and contributing ideas. He is gaining an understanding of many different aspects of the business. Ten years later, he's also the heir apparent as the successor in this successful small company.

Questions to Assess Flexibility and Adaptability

Q: Describe a time when you had to change your plans to accommodate someone else at work.
  • How did you feel about that?

Q: Tell me about a time when something at work was changing.
  • How have you adapted to the change?
  • How did you feel about the change?

Q: Relate a time when you wanted something at work to remain the same, but others didn't.
  - What did you do?
  - How did you feel about that?

Q: Describe a time when you had to learn something new.
  - How did you feel about that?
  - How have you adapted to the new system?

Q: Tell me about a time when you had trouble adjusting to a change.
  - What did you find difficult?

Q: Give me an example of a time when you were flexible.

Q: Give me an example of a time when you weren't very flexible.

Q: Tell me about a time when you had to reconsider how to interact or behave because you weren't getting the results you required.

Q: Were there any behaviors that you had to abandon that worked for you in a previous job that didn't work in a new job?
  - How did you know these behaviors didn't or wouldn't work in your new job?

For managers or leaders:

Q: Tell me about a time as a manager that you found it necessary to bend the rules.
  - What did you do?
  - Why did you do it?
  - How did you feel about it?

Q: Tell me about a time when you were flexible and accommodated the needs of someone on your staff.
  - How did you feel about that?

Q: As a manager, have you ever been flexible and later regretted it?

Q: What types of behaviors did you need to develop when you transitioned from worker to supervisor?

- From manager to director?

Q: Were there any behaviors that you had to abandon that worked for you in a previous role that didn't work in a new role?

- How did you know these behaviors didn't or wouldn't work in your new role?

Q: Was there ever a time when you changed roles or jobs or organizations that you had to let go of behaviors that contributed to your success in past situations?

KEY POINTS TO CONSIDER WHEN ASSESSING ANSWERS

With all the changes that take place in the workplace, candidates should be able to give you concrete examples of times when they had to be flexible. Asking the follow-up question "How did you feel about that?" is an important way to assess the candidate's underlying assumptions about change. Is the candidate someone who enjoys change, or does he like things to remain the same? Look for a picture to emerge about how the candidate views change. Just as with all the competencies, the job will dictate whether or not the competency is important. Being rigid and following a set pattern, schedule, or method may certainly be desirable in some jobs. In fact, being too flexible in some positions may be a detriment. Carefully match the competencies with the job. If flexibility is important, listen for evidence that the candidate is indeed flexible.

Consider this answer to the question "Tell me about a time when you had to adjust to a change at work": "Well, just recently, we changed the procedure for receiving large orders. We used to have two people check in the order. One would check the computer system and verify the order against the packing list, and the other person would check for the merchandise. Now, one person has to do both jobs. So, I had to learn how to use the computer system where the electronic packing lists and orders are stored." The interviewer then asked the follow-up question "How do you feel about that?" and gained the following information: "Well, I don't like it. It's so much easier to do it the other way. It's confusing to find everything on the computer and also go and check the order." Another follow-up question provides even more information about the situation: "How are you adapting to this change?" "Well, I'm doing okay. My supervisor said that I had the fewest discrepancies and also had the fastest check-in speed, so my numbers are very good. Our department measures speed and accuracy of order check-in." So it's possible to dislike the change yet be able to adapt quite well. This answer gives the interviewer important information. If the candidate had said, "I'm adapting okay," the interviewer wouldn't have enough information to evaluate the candidate's position and would need to ask for concrete measures. Also, remember that additional examples will enable the interviewer to determine whether the candidate generally dislikes change, yet adapts well, or whether this is an isolated example. It's important to acquire this information if the job that you're interviewing candidates for requires lots of change and flexibility.

In addition, employees, and especially managers and leaders, should understand that different jobs and roles might require different sets of behaviors. If they are aware that different roles or jobs require different behaviors, probe to discover how they became aware of the need to adapt. Were they able to read the environment or the people and realize that they had to adapt their behavior? Or did someone have to point out the need for a different set of behaviors? Preferably the candidate determined the need for different behaviors by observing others in a similar role, by assessing people's reactions, and by anticipating differences. This internal compass would lead to flexible and adaptable behavior without the need for someone to point it out. If someone must point it out, the person may have already lost credibility or have a performance problem.

Asking a candidate interviewing for a managerial or leadership position about examples of when she accommodated others or when she felt it necessary to bend the rules gives you important insight into the candidate's flexibility. You should assess the answers you receive against the fit within your organization. These questions involve judgment issues that you'll need to evaluate against the landscape of your organization. For example, is the manager's example about bending rules in favor of satisfying customers? The judgment portion of the question is separate from the issue of flexibility. If you're attempting to determine whether someone is flexible, the candidate should be able to give evidence where she demonstrated flexibility in her thinking and decision making and acted in a flexible way.

FIGURE 7.1 **Personal Influence—Influencing Self at a Glance**		
	PROS	**CONS**
Self-Confidence	• Gives realistic description of use of abilities • Gives examples of taking proactive steps in difficult situations • Tone, speech, and other nonverbal behaviors indicate belief in self • Can articulate weaknesses in a manner that indicates self-improvement • Is willing to admit need for help	• Is too fearful to reveal a weakness or ask for assistance • Cannot give examples of actions in difficult situations • Tone, speech, and other nonverbal behaviors indicate lack of belief in self • Makes all-encompassing statements regarding abilities that reflects arrogance • Makes statements that devalue others in the organization
Initiative and Accountability	• Gives concrete examples of independent actions to improve work • Takes responsibility for outcomes of actions • Demonstrates creative actions to solve problems or workplace issues • Blames self when actions do not produce desired results	• Is unable to give examples of actions taken except when directed by others • Blames others or system when actions do not produce results • Uses system as an excuse for inaction

(continued)

FIGURE 7.1 *Continued*

	PROS	CONS
Goal Orientation	• Gives concrete examples of meeting goals • Seeks help if not meeting goals • Seeks clarification of goals and process to meet goals • Is open to coaching or learning from others who reach goals to improve performance	• Rationalizes behavior when goals are unmet • Attacks the goals or standards as unrealistic if not met • Blames others if goals are unmet • Uses excuses such as lack of resources if goals are unmet
Optimism	• Gives examples that emphasize the positive factors • Discusses ideas in terms of possibilities or achievement • Can give examples of things learned from taking risks even if project failed • Discusses failure in terms of what was learned	• Gives examples that emphasize negative factors • Discusses ideas in terms of why they won't work or can't be achieved • Sees projects or ideas as overwhelming • Demonstrates reluctance to try new things
Flexibility	• Can describe alternative solutions to problems • Gives examples of learning new methods or processes • Gives examples of accommodating others • Gives examples of when abandoned own solutions to accommodate others	• Seeks only one solution to a problem, then abandons it • Resists learning new things • Is slow to accept change; doesn't see value in change • Wants to go back to the way it used to be • Describes a narrow comfort range

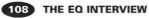

Endnotes

1. Scott Beagrie, "How to . . . Build Up Self-Confidence," *Personnel Today,* September 26, 2006, 31.
2. Robert Simons, "Control in an Age of Empowerment," *Harvard Business Review* 73, 2 (March 1995): 80.
3. Ian Broadmore, "Self-Confidence: Top 10 Tips," *Training and Coaching Today,* October 2006, 21.
4. Simons, "Control in an Age of Empowerment."
5. W. Keith Campbell, Adam S. Goodie, and Joshua D. Foster, "Narcissism, Confidence, and Risk Attitude," *Journal of Behavioral Decision Making* 17, 4 (October 2004): 297.
6. Simons, "Control in an Age of Empowerment."
7. T.L. Stanley, "Managing Your Team," *SuperVision* 67, 6 (June 2006): 10.
8. M. Seligman, *Learned Optimism* (New York: Simon and Schuster, 1998).
9. J.M. George and K. Bettenhausen, "Understanding Prosocial Behavior, Sales Performance, and Turnover: A Group Level Analysis in a Service Context," *Journal of Applied Psychology* 75 (1990): 698–709.
10. Todd Humber, "Emotional Intelligence," *Canadian HR Reporter* 15, 16 (September 23, 2002): G1.
11. Seligman, *Learned Optimism.*
12. Adele B. Lynn, *The EQ Difference* (New York: AMACOM, 2004).
13. W.H. Bergquist, *The Postmodern Organization: Mastering the Art of Irreversible Change* (San Francisco: Jossey-Bass, 1993).

CHAPTER 8

Personal Influence: Influencing Others

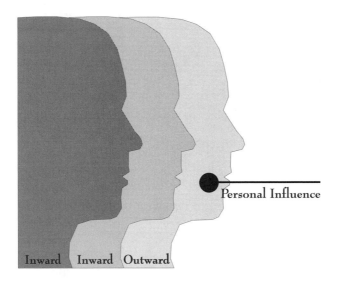

Personal Influence

Inward   Inward   Outward

Competency 1—Leading Others
Competency 2—Creating a Positive Work Climate
Competency 3—Getting Results Through Others

nfluencing others lies at the heart of many jobs. In today's work environments, influence is exercised at many levels—boss to subordinate, peer to peer within departments, peer to peer across departments, and even grassroots bottom-up influence, where empowered workers and teams make decisions and influence management to act upon their decisions. No less important is the need to exert positive influence with customers, vendors, and patients as we manage these crucial relationships. Influence, once the primary bailiwick of management, now often belongs to everyone within the organization. In many environments, the person with the strongest skills for a particular task or project emerges as the leader. In this way, leaders emerge and retreat as the work demands. Whether or not you own the title of leader, many jobs require you to influence others. Influence sends a message of respect, results in actions that are voluntary, and yields better quality. When you need to get things done through other people over whom you have no power, influence is often the best or only choice to get the job done.[1] Influence combines many of the competencies we've talked about thus far. In this case, however, they converge into three competencies:

1. *Leading others,* which is the ability to get others to follow you;

2. *Creating a positive work culture;* and

3. *Getting results through others.*

Competency 1: Leading Others

In a pure sense, someone's leadership competence can be measured by determining whether others follow. The idea that it takes followers to define a leader proves worthy, especially with a candidate applying for a position of leadership. Asking questions aimed at uncovering times when people follow would indicate whether or not the candidate successfully leads others. There is no doubt that Hitler, Christ, and Martin Luther King, Jr., were all leaders because of the sheer volumes of people that were followers. We recognize, of course, that if one is to be an effective leader, many other competencies must also be in place. But at this point, the interviewer and hiring manager must look for evidence that the candidate capably gets people to follow her.

Consider these examples: Jeanette's passion about music and theater abounds. She lives in a small town more than a three-hour drive from the nearest city. She decided that three hours was too far to drive to enjoy her passion. So, she began to plant seeds in her community about starting a local theater group. In the four years after she first aired her idea of starting a local theater group, Jeanette has assembled dozens of actors and artists, many sponsors, and throngs of fans who participate in a robust summer theater series.

In another example, Brien, a serious student of Deming's quality concepts, decided to create a Deming study group to learn and discuss the application of Deming's teaching. Twenty years later, this small study group, now called CoREM—the Council on Realizing Excellence in Management—still meets monthly. The group organizes guest speakers who present ideas for discussion, book reviews, case studies, and new concepts to a group of interested learners. Brien still holds a leadership role in this quiet nonprofit, which offers all of its programs free of charge.

In yet another example, Gerard believed that the small company he worked for wasted thousands of dollars in time and materials due to improper training. He said that when he came on board three years ago, no training program existed for new employees. After struggling for six months to learn the job, Gerard decided that no one should have to go through what he went through. He asked all of his coworkers to help him document the training process. He convinced them that by documenting and helping new people learn the job, everyone's life would improve because of fewer reworks, less frustration, and a greater amount of money to be divided in the profit-sharing program. Most people contributed, and Gerard created a training program for new hires that the company uses today. In each of these examples, these people created followers. The ability to get people to follow is a critical component of influencing others.

Questions to Assess Leading Others

Q: Tell me about a time you had an idea and you got other people to follow you.

- What did you do?

Q: Describe a time when others relied on you and followed your lead.

Q: Tell me about a time when you were able to influence others.
- How did you do it?
- How did you feel about influencing others?

Q: Describe a time when you took charge of a situation.

Q: Tell me about a time when others looked to you for direction.
- What did you do?
- How did you feel about that?

For managers and leaders:

Q: How do you get people to follow you?
- What do you do?
- How do you influence them?

Q: Tell me about a time when someone was resisting you.
- What did you do?

Q: Describe a time when you were able to get people to follow you on a controversial issue.

Q: Tell me about a time when you united your followers around an issue.

Q: Describe a time when you influenced people to follow you when you did not have positional authority.

Q: Give me an example of when you influenced your peers.

Q: Give me an example of when you influenced your boss.

KEY POINTS TO CONSIDER WHEN ASSESSING ANSWERS

The candidate should be able to provide examples of times when she emerged as a leader. Look for examples when the candidate deliberately demonstrated leadership and also for examples of when the candidate emerged as a leader because others sought out her knowledge, skill, or interest in a particular task or subject. When a candidate deliberately demonstrates leadership, she chooses to lead. All three of the examples provided above demonstrate deliberate leadership.

However, depending on the role and the job that you as the interviewer or hiring manager must fill, it is also useful to determine whether others seek out the candidate as a leader. When others ask a candidate to provide leadership, this demonstrates that the candidate possesses some quality or expertise that others require. When asked to give an example of when others followed his lead, one candidate answered in a humble, quiet demeanor, "Well, there was a very tense situation with a huge customer. We were supposed to deliver something on spec and we missed the deadline and didn't manufacture it up to spec. The customer was threatening to pull his business. (The customer accounts for 40 percent of our revenues.) Joe came to me and asked if I would be willing to meet with the team to address the situation. I have a long history and a good reputation with this customer. So, I did. The team took my recommendations and we were able to retain the customer. Joe also asked me if I would stay involved with the team for a while to make sure that we maintain the customer's confidence. It's been about a year and things are running really well." This candidate clearly demonstrated that he had expertise, and he influenced the team through his reputation and skill.

When you're evaluating a candidate's influence, remember that charisma and assertiveness don't necessarily make a person influential. Influence comes in many different sizes and styles. Look for the type that will make a good fit with the position and your organization. Someone can exercise leadership with a very quiet and unassuming style. Look for results and evidence, not for charm.

When interviewing to fill a managerial or leadership position, assess the methods candidates use to influence people. Obviously, they have positional authority; however, look for examples of how they influence people beyond the use of positional authority. If the only answer a candidate can give you is, "I just told Jim he had to do it," I would be concerned that the candidate isn't aware of the other methods of influence. Probe deeply to give the candidate an opportunity to tell you about his tactics and methods for influencing followers. In *The World's Most Powerful Leadership Principle,* James Hunter describes a positive method as "the skill of influencing people to enthusiastically work toward goals identified as being for the common good."[2] To accomplish enthusiastic support and garner a following, leaders must engage people, value them, honor their ideas through listening, and help them to feel important. They must express gratitude and display caring. However, leaders must also display competence. Watch for signs of these behaviors in the answers that you gather.

Questions aimed at influencing peers as well as the boss give you valuable insight into the candidate's method of influence when positional authority doesn't exist. One candidate, when asked about gaining a peer's cooperation said, "I went to our boss and let him deal with it." Again, the interviewer gains important information. Another telling example came when a candidate was asked about resistance. He responded, "I don't believe in playing games with people. We're here to get the job done, so whenever I say to do something, I expect people to do it or I tell them they can go somewhere else."

Competency 2: Creating a Positive Work Climate

The culture created by the leader directly affects employee satisfaction, retention, creativity, and innovation. One of management's fundamental tasks is to provide the environment and methods that encourage employee initiative.[3] Climate also affects coworkers' moods and attitudes, with positive mood increasing worker effectiveness and retention.[4] Also, a positive climate helps to reduce job stress. Job stress costs U.S. industry $300 billion annually in increased health-care costs and employee absenteeism, so there are many benefits to creating a positive climate, including financial savings, greater job satisfaction, and recruiting advantages for companies.[5] Employees report that stress negatively impacts relationships with coworkers, productivity, and decision making.[6] Assessing a candidate's ability to create a positive working culture is often quite desirable when the interviewer or hiring manager is screening candidates for positional leaders. Although climate and culture are certainly affected by events and circumstances beyond the immediate leader's control, the immediate leader does have control over much of what people experience every day in the workplace. In fact, when low employee morale exists, generally, it can be traced to dysfunctional leadership.[7]

When interviewing a candidate for a leadership position, the interviewer or hiring manager should determine whether or not the candidate assumes responsibility for the workplace climate in her unit or department. Furthermore, determine whether the candidate links leadership behavior to morale issues. The leader has a dual role in understanding his behavioral impact on climate and culture. The leader monitors the actions of his work group to ensure that members treat others with respect and civility. Workplace incivility reinforces isolation and reduces workers' responses and choices, including ideas, creativity, and participation in decision making.[8] The leader must also recognize which of his personal traits and characteristics lead to low morale, including micromanagement, procrastination on decisions, perfectionism, not listening, and overpromising. For example, an immediate leader may not be able to change the impact of negative market conditions, but she can control whether or not people's ideas or concerns are heard.

Consider these examples. Fourteen financial professionals in the Private Equity Department reported to Markus. It didn't take long for new professionals to get the word—if you wanted someone to mentor you and help you succeed in Private Equity at this financial institution, then work for Markus. His reputation as a great teacher placed high expectations on everyone who reported to him. Everyone was expected to share information with one another and to teach one another. He threw elaborate celebrations when members of his group accomplished special certifications. He also went out of his way to make sure everyone got a piece of the juicy assignments. He believed that if everyone shared in the good assignments, then everyone would learn higher-level skills. While other areas of the Private Equity Department were quiet and stilted, Markus's area was lively and interactive, with frequent celebrations.

Jody managed a retail establishment at a local chain store. There were three such stores within a ten-mile radius. Jody's reputation as a firm, fun, and fair manager earned her the nickname "Coach." She went out of her way to accommodate people and set high expectations for performance, and she believed in having fun. People would often transfer from the other store locations to work at Jody's location. Her turnover rate was the lowest of all the stores in her district.

Questions to Assess Creating a Positive Work Climate

For leaders and managers:

Q: Describe the climate or culture of your present department.

Q: What specific steps do you take to set the tone within your department?

Q: How is the climate within your department different from that of other areas within your company?

Q: What evidence do you have that you've created a positive climate or culture?

Q: Describe the ideal climate of a department.
  • What actions do you think a leader must take to create an ideal climate?

Q: Tell me about a time when your staff was not very energized.
  • What did you do?

Q: Tell me about a time when someone expressed concerns about the working climate of your department.
  • What did you do?

Q: Describe a situation when an employee was disrupting the climate you were trying to establish.
  • What did you do?

For employees:

Q: Describe a positive working climate.
  • What would it feel like?
  • What do you do to create a positive working climate every day?

Q: Give me some examples of what you do to ensure that your coworkers have a positive day.

Q: Give me an example of some actions you've taken with a negative coworker.

- What have you done to create a more positive working relationship with this person?

Q: How do you support your supervisor in creating a positive climate in your work unit?

KEY POINTS TO CONSIDER WHEN ASSESSING ANSWERS

Generally, these questions are for leaders or managers, who should be able to give you answers that indicate that they recognize their responsibility for creating a positive climate within their work group. Good leaders visualize and articulate the culture they expect to create in their work units. That vision should be consistent and fit within your company or organization. In addition, candidates should be able to outline specific steps that they have taken to create a positive climate with their staff. The answers that you gain should give you a good indication of whether or not the candidate even considers climate to be his responsibility. Although organizational issues, market conditions, and other factors influence employee morale and satisfaction, so does the direct leader's action. Probe further to determine whether the leader recognizes that he controls certain factors, and look for evidence of how the leader acts. It's also helpful to ask for more than one example. If a person has held more than one leadership position or has worked in multiple companies or organizations, asking for multiple examples gives the interviewer more insight into how the candidate sets the tone or climate when in a leadership role.

Some leaders tie the climate to the corporate values of teamwork or respect. Some develop their own set of operating behaviors for their department or team. The key point here is that leaders should have a clear vision, should establish guidelines for interacting that support the vision, should have clearly communicated what's expected, and should act in a manner that is consistent with this vision. The candidate should also be able to give evidence of the positive culture she created. Is her overturn rate lower than average? Are there opinion surveys or satisfaction surveys that call out her department as unusually high scoring? Even anecdotal evidence can support her claims. One working supervisor was able to describe a very positive culture; when asked for evidence, she said, "Well, this isn't something that you can measure, but when my husband was diagnosed with cancer, my employees all got together. They took it upon themselves to divide up some of my work. They said that while my husband was sick, they were all going to pitch in and try to relieve me of some of my tasks. In addition, they left me a written report every day letting me know what they were able to complete. Everyone worked together on this. It was great." Obviously, this person did something to engender this kind of support.

Another point worth noting involves the energy of the work unit. Energy and mood are contagious, and the leader sets the tone. Is the candidate aware that he or she can take actions to increase the energy level of the group? One candidate said that she noticed that her staff was getting weary during a particularly busy time in the dead of winter. She decided to have a summer luau party one Monday afternoon. It was a total surprise, and she purposely chose Monday. She said the energy and high spirit created by the luau lasted all week.

Also, ask about how the leader would address a negative or resistant employee. Will the candidate act to defend the culture he is creating? Will he teach and mentor employees to support the culture? Sometimes, leaders do a good job of envisioning and articulating a positive culture, but they get stymied when someone resists. Perhaps they lack the skill or the courage to address resistance. One leader gave evidence of a very positive culture that he created; then a new person entered the work unit, and her manipulative and backstabbing behavior destroyed what he had created. He said in the interview, "I learned how one person could destroy everything I worked hard to build." When the interviewer probed with "What did you do when you realized this was happening?" the candidate responded, "Well, there wasn't much I could do, she was very strong willed." This sense of helplessness speaks volumes. Assuming that the manipulative person was hired by this leader, the situation would even be worse. The leader didn't take actions to defend the culture he created, nor did he initially hire someone who would fit into the culture.

Although the responsibility for creating a positive climate rests primarily with the leader, employee actions speak volumes. Questioning a candidate about climate and her role in it gives the interviewer or hiring manager insight into the candidate's self-leadership skills. Does the candidate realize that all people have a role in setting climate or tone? Does she take actions to create a positive climate with peers and others? Ask a candidate some questions to assess what actions and responsibility she takes to set the tone. One candidate said, "It's not my job to worry about whether or not my coworkers are having a good day. That's my boss's job." On the contrary, if each employee concerned herself with whether or not her coworkers were having a good day, morale problems would go away. Also, serving internal customers (coworkers) requires the attitude that each person manages his behavior to create a positive experience for the people he encounters. Be sure to probe; questions such as these will often elicit simple answers such as, "I'm real easy to get along with. Everyone likes me." That may be true, but that answer lacks clarity. Dig deeper for specific examples of how the candidate behaves. That characteristic engenders a positive climate.

Competency 3: Getting Results Through Others

Setting a positive climate may be great for morale and retention, but ultimately, a leader must deliver results. Achieving high morale but accomplishing nothing is simply not an option in today's corporate world. The interviewer must assess whether or not a candidate achieves important goals through people. The best leader will, of course, deliver on both of these important qualities. Assessing a person's ability to influence others requires the interviewer or hiring manager to ask for specific examples of achievements as well as the methods the leader used to influence others. Leaders can get results by using some very negative methods, such as threats and fear. A leader can also get results by doing much of the work himself, or by relying heavily on a few key people. Yet, these methods often lead to negative consequences, such as turnover, in the long run. It's important to balance your questions by asking both about the results that the leader achieved and about *how* the results were achieved. One study indicated that managers who used positive tactics to influence people, as measured by their ability to interact effectively and gain the approval and support of coworkers, were compensated 29 percent more than their counterparts, indicating that organizations place higher value on *how* people get results than on the results themselves.[9]

Leadership also means influencing peers, vendors, customers, and others—all instances where the candidate has no direct authority. Depending on the position you are hiring for, you may want to evaluate the candidate's ability to get results through others when the candidate does not have positional authority. In higher executive levels, such as directors or above, jobs often require working with and influencing peers to implement enterprisewide solutions. At these levels, methods such as building close working relationships, inviting collaboration, creating open and authentic agendas, and helping others look like heroes produce influence and results.

Consider these examples: Freda always looked frazzled. She was constantly rushing and in constant motion. She would jump from one fire to another. Many times, her staff sat around waiting for her to come to their aid or tell them what to do. They lacked clear direction. Also, they required key information from Freda. So they could go only so far in their work, and then they would have to wait until Freda came to their side to provide some type of guidance. Freda worked hard. But she failed to exercise leadership. Although she had the title, she showed no signs of getting results through others. Unfortunately, Freda's department results reflected her inability to get things done through others.

In another example, Sarah's top priority was making sure her staff understood their job expectations. Also, she took time to establish measures and gave people feedback on their performance. She believed creating the right atmosphere and then providing any kind of support that she could to help people reach their goals produced results. She was right. Sarah's unit scored the highest results on the balanced scorecard measures for the three most recent quarters.

Questions to Assess Getting Results Through Others

For managers or leaders:

Q: Describe some of the results you've achieved in your area within the past year.

- How did you achieve those results?

Q: In what areas did you fall short of delivering the results you wanted to deliver?

- Why did you fall short?
- What could you have done differently?

Q: Describe how you typically get results from other people.

Q: Tell me how you set goals for your staff.
- Give me an example of a time when someone wasn't meeting a goal.
- What did you do?

Q: Has there ever been a time when no matter what you did, someone was unable to reach a goal?
- What did you do?

Q: What have you done to share your expectations with your department?

Q: Have you ever set a goal too low?
- What did you do?

Q: Tell me about a time when someone was resisting you, your ideas, or your authority.
- What did you do?

Q: Tell me about a time that you were wrong in the way that you addressed an employee situation.

Q: As a manager, tell me about a time when you didn't have enough resources to do the job.
- What did you do?

For employees:

Q: Describe a situation when your actions helped others achieve results or goals.

KEY POINTS TO CONSIDER WHEN ASSESSING ANSWERS

When interviewing candidates for leadership positions, be sure to establish evidence that they use established performance-management techniques. Good performance management requires the leader to establish clear expectations, measure performance, clearly communicate expectations and measures, monitor employee performance, and give feedback throughout the performance cycle. Through your discussions with the candidate, you should be able to determine what the candidate does to clarify expectations, how the candidate checks or monitors results, and whether or not the candidate gives regular performance feedback. But the manner in which the leader executes this process is critical. Use the interview process to determine *how* the candidate engages the employee in the performance-management system. Organizations with effective performance-management processes create a culture of dialogue. Leaders must encourage pervasive two-way communication, through which individuals and groups question, challenge, interpret, and clarify goals and engage in regular performance dialogue to ensure that employees' actions are aligned with the organization's goals.[10]

For example, from the candidate's answers, do you get a sense that the process is collaborative? In addition, what is the tone of the discussions the candidate is conveying? Does the candidate see herself as a partner for achieving goals? Does the candidate offer employees help and resources to reach goals? Does the candidate see herself as a mentor or coach to help people achieve goals? When asked about goals and the role the manager plays, one candidate stated, "Look, I put it out there in no uncertain terms. Everyone knows what I expect. I'm not there to hold anyone's hand. If they can't deliver, I have to cut my losses." This candidate might deliver clearly defined goals, but it seems that the process stops there. Although we're not suggesting that an emotionally intelligent leader coddle someone, a bit of coaching would certainly be in order. Why? Because people's performance improves when the leader actively gives performance feedback and has built a coaching relationship with the employee.

It's also interesting to examine how a candidate addresses resistant or reluctant employees. Did the candidate immediately push back or give the employee an ultimatum? Did he give up and get other people to cover for the resistant employee? Or did he give clear feedback, listen to the employee, involve the employee in problem solving, and offer support, additional training, or other resources to overcome the performance difficulty? Listen carefully to distill the tone of the employee discussions. There is one thing you can count on as a leader: eventually, someone, somewhere, will resist your ideas, suggestions, or goals. Learning what the candidate does to influence a person who resists gives the interviewer critical information. Look for answers that suggest that the candidate worked up front to build the relationship; included the employee's input and collaborated with the employee on the ideas, projects, or goals; and asked for employee feedback and listened to employee concerns. True influence is in the details and the tone.

Sometimes, however, even a leader who employed all the right methods encounters a situation in which a person is unwilling or unable to meet the demands of the job. In this case, the leader must courageously take the next step—progressive discipline. The interviewer must determine whether the candidate gave the employee in question fair and ample coaching and counseling, and then whether the leader addressed the situation in an honorable manner—even if it ended in termination. If a leader fails to address performance problems, ultimately, he can lose influence with others on his team, because by accepting lowers standards for one person, he lowers the expectations for everyone.

To determine how a candidate gets results when he has no positional authority, be sure to direct your questions specifically to that point. Ask, "How do you typically get results from *peers?*" or "Tell me about a time when a *peer* resisted you, or your ideas. What did you do?" Here again, the candidate should give answers that describe collaborative approaches. Did the candidate recognize the need for strong peer-to-peer relationships? Did she ask for input on ideas, projects, or goals that affected peers? Was the candidate open to feedback, and did she listen to concerns? Influence is made of building blocks. A candidate's awareness of the process of influencing others will be evident in the manner in which she describes her interactions.

FIGURE 8.1 **Personal Influence—Influencing Others at a Glance**

	PROS	CONS
Leading Others	• Gives concrete examples of others seeking out her opinion or guidance • Gives concrete examples of times when she directed other people's actions • Gives concrete examples of when others followed her lead	• Gives vague or unrealistic examples of incidences of others following • Gives an exaggerated portrait of others' reliance on her • Is unable to give examples of others seeking out her opinion or guidance
Creating a Positive Culture	• Gives examples of small gestures toward others that contribute to positive culture • Speaks in positive terms about the mission and the people in the organization • Expresses responsibility for the culture and gives specific examples • Recognizes a role in reaching out to win over negative peers	• Places all the responsibility on others to create a positive workplace; minimizes own role • Blames others for lack of positive culture • Espouses a negative view of organization and people
Getting Results Through Others	• Clearly sets goals for the department • Gives examples of articulating goals to others • Coaches people who are falling short of goals	• Does not give clear goals and directions • Cannot give examples of clearly setting expectations • Cannot give examples

	PROS	CONS
	• Gives both positive and negative feedback regarding goals and behaviors	of helping people understand or reach goals • Cannot give examples of giving balanced feedback for people who aren't reaching goals

FIGURE 8.1 *Continued*

Endnotes

1. Kim Barnes, "Influence and Power," *Executive Excellence* (September 2002): 9.
2. James Hunter, *The World's Most Powerful Leadership Principle* (New York: Crown Business, 2004).
3. John G. Smale, "Committed People: The Key to Managing Change," *Review of Business* 7, 2 (Fall 1985): 31.
4. Sigal G. Barsade, "The Ripple Effect: Emotional Contagion and Its Influence on Group Behavior," *Administrative Science Quarterly* 47 (December 2002): 644.
5. Gail Kelley, "Got a Happy Office? Then Shout It Out: Psychologist Group Is Recognizing Best Work Environments," *Knight Ridder Tribune Business News,* July 5, 2007, 1.
6. "New Poll: Stress Can Limit Emotional Intelligence and Workplace Success; American Workers Take Notice: Stress Is Causing Professional Problems on the Promotional Front," *PR Newswire,* July 30, 2007.
7. Richard Wright, "When Your Worst Enemy Is You," *Profit* 26, 1 (March 2007): 55.
8. C.M. Pearson, L.M. Andersson, and J.W. Wegner, "When Workers Flout Convention: A Study of Workplace Incivility," *Human Relations* 54, 11 (2001): 1387–1419.
9. "New Research Proves Interpersonal Skills Make High-Performing Managers; Study Shows That Building Effective Relationships Is Critical to Managerial Success," *Business Wire,* August 31, 2005, 1.
10. Eleana Rodriquez, "Achieving Outstanding Performance Through a 'Culture of Dialogue,' " *Workspan* 45, 9 (September 2002): 24.

CHAPTER 9

Mastery of Purpose and Vision

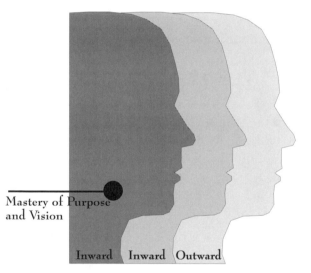

Mastery of Purpose
and Vision

Inward   Inward   Outward

Competency 1—Understanding One's Purpose and Values
Competency 2—Taking Actions Toward One's Purpose
Competency 3—Authenticity

Mastery of purpose and vision is defined as the ability to bring authenticity to one's life and live out one's intentions and values. A clearly defined purpose and values serve as an internal compass to assist a person to quickly discern what is important and what types of actions and behaviors support his purpose. Mastery of purpose and vision serves as a strong enabling factor in helping a person manage emotions and relationships. It aids decision making when an individual faces difficult choices. It also helps a person stay motivated to behave in a manner consistent with his values and intentions. Mastery of purpose and vision is the foundation on which emotional intelligence is based. All of the other areas build on this foundation. Three competencies emerge in this area of emotional intelligence:

1. *Understanding one's purpose and values,* which is to understand one's life purpose and values;

2. *Taking actions toward one's purpose,* which means to take action or steps to live one's purpose; and

3. *Authenticity,* which means to live authentically when purpose, values, actions, and motives are all aligned.

Competency 1: Understanding One's Purpose and Values

A clearly defined purpose and values set the direction for our interaction with the world. As I asked in *The EQ Difference,* paraphrased here. "At the end of your life, will your life script read as a carefully scripted book with each chapter intentionally supporting the next, or will it appear unintentional and haphazard?"[1] Since we spend at least forty hours a week at work, work constitutes a large chapter of our lives. Does the work you've chosen to do support your purpose and values, or is it in conflict? Is the organization that you've chosen aligned with your values? All candidates in the quest for the right job should consider these questions for themselves. These questions help candidates determine whether they have chosen the right path. However, hiring managers and interviewers have much to gain with these types of questions as well. These questions speak to fit.

By asking a few choice questions, the interviewer or hiring manager can determine whether the candidate will find satisfaction in the job for which he is applying. These questions serve to help the candidate and the interviewer determine whether the job suits the candidate. Is this the type of job where a person can experience "flow"? The term "flow," as applied to work, created by Mihaly Csikszentmihalyi, means being in an optimal state of work, where our challenge and our available time, interest, and skill are perfectly aligned.[2] By uncovering purpose, we assess our natural gifts, talents, and skills and work to match these with available challenges. When interviewing a candidate, we don't generally recommend that the interviewer or hiring manager ask a person to describe his purpose or values. Instead, we suggest gaining an understanding of when the candidate feels most inspired and connected to work.

Consider the following example. Vivian described her favorite job as the one she has right now. She said that she works in a very fast-paced position, so she doesn't ever get bored. She trains others, which she said appeals to her sense of helping people. She said she really loves seeing people learn new things, so she gets positive reinforcement when the people she trains acquire new skills. She says that the training makes use of her best skills, organizing information and communicating it in a way that people understand. Her days just fly by because she finds her work so aligned with who she is and what's important to her.

In another example, Ernest is miserable. He says that he loves being outdoors, working and being around people and doing things with his hands. Currently he commutes two hours to the city each day and works as a programmer. Although he works with a team of people, they meet only once per week to review their progress; otherwise, he works alone in a cubical all day. Ernest describes his days as serving time. It's no wonder. He has somehow crafted a job for himself that is completely contrary to what seems ideal to him.

Questions to Assess Understanding One's Purpose and Values

Q: Describe a time when you were lost in your work in a good way—when time just flew by and you were totally absorbed in what you were doing.

Q: Tell me about a time when you felt bored at work.

Q: Describe your ideal job.

Q: Describe the worst possible job for you.

Q: What type of work would you find most inspiring?

KEY POINTS TO CONSIDER WHEN ASSESSING ANSWERS

By asking these questions, the interviewer should get a picture of the type of work most aligned with the candidate's interests. Of course, it would be very useful if you asked these questions before you described the job. If the candidate knows what the job entails in advance, the candidate may answer the questions to suit the position. So, as the interviewer, arrange your discussion so that you ask these questions before you describe the position or job duties. The question about being lost in one's work, earlier described as flow, helps the interviewer understand the kind of work that resonates with the candidate. One candidate stated that the worst possible job for him would be a position where he would have little or no help in solving problems and be expected to interact with angry people all day. Well, the technical support opening required a great deal of independent problem solving with little direction. It also required almost constant interface with irate users. So, fit may be an issue in this case. Another candidate described feeling bored and disliked attending meetings. If the particular culture at the hiring company and the position required the candidate to attend meetings, this misalignment may be cause for concern. Getting to know a candidate on this level enables better hiring decisions.

As for the question "What type of work would you find most inspiring?" we're not suggesting that you should necessarily eliminate a candidate based on the response to this question, but it does give you information to consider. Let's say that you're interviewing candidates for an accounting job at a financial institution and the candidate states that the job they would find most inspiring would be working with children—a far cry from accounting. Does that mean he would make a poor accountant? No, so this statement is not a factor that should eliminate this candidate as a potential hire, but if you have another candidate who loves numbers and gives evidence of that, the latter may be a better fit in terms of job satisfaction. A study in the *Journal of Vocational Behavior* cited a positive correlation between emotional intelligence and job satisfaction.[3] People who are able to articulate what type of work they find inspiring are demonstrating a level of awareness that should be taken into consideration when assessing fit.

Competency 2: Taking Actions Toward One's Purpose

Understanding one's purpose and values doesn't necessarily translate to action. Action requires—well, just that—action. So determining what actions people take to align and support their purpose and values proves to be a fruitful line of questioning in an interview situation. It not only requires an understanding of what's important in one's life; it also requires motivation to seek and fulfill it. When someone takes actions to advance his purpose, he feels a sense of control or mastery over a situation. That feeling empowers people, and fulfillment follows. That's not to say that the path will always be smooth, but the research suggests that people are happiest when they are on a path they have determined, even if that path has some obstacles.[4] Taking the easy road to nowhere doesn't seem to lead to fulfillment. And taking the difficult road to where you don't care to be certainly seems like a wrong turn.

Consider these cases: Jim was always good at math and science, so he decided to major in engineering. He graduated with his engineering degree and worked as an engineer for eight years. Eventually he discovered that engineering was devoid of the people contact he craved. He also sensed that his life lacked a sense of meaning. He decided to go back to school to pursue a medical degree, even though it cost him in terms of both time and dollars. He works now as a family practice doctor. Twenty years later, he still feels inspired and energized by his decision to follow his heart.

Frank pursued a degree in computer science because his parents, his guidance counselor, and even the media steered him in that direction. The allure of plentiful and well-paying jobs sealed his fate. Ten years later, he discovered that he's miserable. Another ten years have passed, and it's confirmed. He's definitely miserable. Now the goal is to put in another ten or fifteen years and make it to retirement.

Granted, sometimes people must make sacrifices because of family obligations or other situations, but sometimes people simply stay stuck. By asking people some probing questions, you can gain a sense of their mastery about their life direction. Since our interviewing questions focus on work, we keep the questions focused there.

Q: How did you decide on your chosen field of endeavor, college major, or line of work?
  • What influenced you?
  • What actions did you take to end up in this field?

Q: What do you like about your chosen field?
  • What do you dislike?

Q: What actions have you taken related to your career that you are pleased you took?
  • What pleases you about your actions?

Q: Have you ever pursued a career-related goal, perhaps a credential or a specific job, only to discover that when you achieved your goal you were disappointed?
  • Tell me about that.

KEY POINTS TO CONSIDER WHEN ASSESSING ANSWERS

Interviewers or hiring managers should ask candidates to give them evidence of deliberate actions leading to specific goals or job paths. In particular, look for evidence of when candidates took actions toward something they found desirable. We recognize that sometimes people simply "fall into" the ideal life path. But once on the ideal path, what actions does the person take to advance on this path? As the interviewer looks for signs of intrinsic motivation toward work, she gains a deeper understanding of the candidate's willingness to pursue interests and goals. The interviewer also discovers what the candidate likes and dislikes. One candidate indicated that he was leaving a particular job because he didn't enjoy it; yet, he was applying for essentially the same type of work. Something seemed amiss, so the interviewer pressed for more details. It turns out that the candidate was asked to leave his job.

We recognize that sometimes people perform jobs just for the money. Jobs sometimes serve as a means to an end, while true fulfillment takes place elsewhere in life. Depending on the candidate's situation, he may not be seeking an ideal job. However, often the candidate can provide evidence of taking action toward his purpose. One candidate applying for a night-turn production job provided a good example. When asked "What actions have you taken toward your career that you were pleased you took?" the candidate answered, "I'm taking one right now by applying for this job. With this job, I'll be working night turn, and that will enable me to take classes during the day and finish my degree."

What about the hoards of people who feel stuck in fields they don't particularly like, but stay because of good pay or convenient hours, or some other personal reason? Should they all be written off at this stage of the interview process? No. The entire interview process looks for the best candidate for the job on many different levels. These questions simply help to determine potential fit and satisfaction. The interviewer or hiring manager may find that these questions better serve some jobs and not others. Alternatively, the interviewer may ask some general questions to determine fit. When given the opportunity, interviewers or hiring managers who hire for skill *and* fit serve the organization better in the long run.

Competency 3: Authenticity

When people's motives, actions, intentions, values, and purpose are aligned, they appear authentic or transparent. In other words, what you see is what you get. No hidden agendas or Machiavellian tendencies emerge when one deals with authentic people. In the workplace, authenticity leads to a high level of trust, which engenders loyalty and honesty. When interacting with people who display authentic behaviors, we feel safe to disclose the truth and to be open about issues, concerns, and problems. Authenticity dissuades yes-people. That makes authenticity quite a desired quality, especially in positions of leadership. Companies who build this mutual sense of respect and trust experience more success. One study of comparable companies in the UK engineering industry stated that companies who build trust were 19 percent more likely to be winning companies in terms of bottom-line worth.[5]

Sometimes authenticity is as simple as honoring commitments and promises. Leaders who make promises they don't keep violate trust.

Leading effectively requires consistency not only in purpose, but also in follow-through.[6] Leaders must constantly be asking themselves, "What commitments have I made to this person?" and "How well am I doing in meeting those commitments?"

Honoring commitments extends to all employees. Peers, coworkers, customers, and patients also expect us to honor our commitments. Authenticity aligns what we say with what we deliver. The interviewing process can test this quality by uncovering evidence that the candidate does or does not deliver on promises.

Sometimes, lack of authenticity comes from conflicted values or goals, not because a person deliberately intends to deceive. When a person's values or goals conflict with the operating values of a particular organization, that person may not appear transparent or open. Why? Because he tries to fit into an organizational culture foreign to his belief system and must constantly monitor his actions. He can't just be himself. Therefore, the organizational fit may be wrong. According to a survey in which employees were asked how strongly they agreed or disagreed with the statement "On my job, I sometimes have to do things that go against my conscience," 20 percent of employees said that they somewhat or strongly agreed.[7] Acting against one's belief system creates a schism in authenticity. On the contrary, when people feel congruence between their individual values and goals and those of the organization, they will be more embedded in the organization.[8] When evaluating a candidate for a leadership position, the interviewer or hiring manager gains valuable insight by determining how well the candidate fits with the organization's cultural values. India's highly successful B. Sathyaseeian describes it thus: "A good leader must have clarity of values. He must know what is most valuable to his life, something that he well never trade off."[9]

Consider the following: Laura is known as the "queen of spin." Her technical skills and productivity are unsurpassed. However, Laura's peers view her as manipulative. They say she spins information to suit the situation and often seems to have hidden agendas.

Ignatius believes that leaders should demonstrate heart. He believes that setting clear expectations, then demonstrating caring and empathy, produce the best results with employees. However, he's working in a company where the operating manifesto is "kick butt and take names." On more than one occasion, Ignatius received negative feedback from his superiors about his "soft" methods. Now Ignatius guards what he says and does. His attempts to be nice on the sly produce a distrustful atmosphere with his bosses. Ignatius feels daily tension as he interacts with both his bosses and his employees.

Questions to Assess Authenticity

Q: Describe a situation where you found yourself in a values conflict.
  - What did you do?

Q: Tell me about a situation at work where you felt that you had to compromise your beliefs or values.

Q: Describe a time when you felt very strongly about something that happened at work—something you considered to be an affront to your values.
  - What did you do?

Q: Tell me how you gain people's trust.
  - What do you do?
  - What actions did you take?

Q: Tell me about a time when you lost someone's trust.

Q: Describe how you know you have honored the commitments that you've made to others.

Q: Tell me about a time when you failed to honor a commitment.

Q: Has there ever been a time when you promised something at work and were unable to deliver it?
  - How did you feel about that?

Q: Tell me about a time when you did less than your fair share at work or you got out of a difficult assignment.
  - How did you feel about that?

KEY POINTS TO CONSIDER WHEN ASSESSING ANSWERS

The questions about values conflicts and compromised beliefs produce useful data. As the interviewer, you'll want to listen to the candidate's willingness to tell you the truth. Sure, everyone wants to present himself as a team player, but what is the candidate willing to disclose? Generally, people who feel strongly about their values can give an example. The interviewer must refrain from judging the candidate's values. Remember, the intention of these questions is to determine whether the candidate will fit in the hiring organization.

When candidates discuss how they gain trust, look for specific actions or behaviors. People skilled at building trust do so by developing relationships, listening to others, responding with empathy, genuinely soliciting input from others, and, of course, contributing fairly. Fair and equal contributions at work, measured by following through with promised and assigned work and honoring commitments, lead to workplace trust.[10]

Most candidates find the question "Tell me about a time when you lost someone's trust" more challenging. Candidates also find "Tell me about a time when you did less than your fair share" difficult to answer. The interviewer may have to prime the candidate to disclose this information. However, if a candidate provides an answer, follow up with "How did you feel about that?" One candidate stated that he felt really lucky to get out of some difficult assignments. When the interviewer probed, she was told, "I don't really care to learn something that I'm probably never going to do again." That answer may be truthful, so you have to be grateful that the candidate was honest. But if the job for which you're interviewing candidates requires the candidate to learn new things that he may not use on a daily basis, fit becomes the issue.

If manipulation and deceit are a candidate's strong points, it's unlikely that these questions will prove useful. We've devoted Chapter 10 to discussing this problem.

FIGURE 9.1 Mastery of Purpose and Vision at a Glance

	PROS	CONS
Understanding Purpose and Values	• Can articulate the type of work that he enjoys • Describes work that is not suitable or inspiring • Gives examples of work that is aligned with his interests and values	• Cannot produce examples of work that he enjoys • Work path indicates bouncing among various jobs with no satisfaction • Dismisses work as something that must be tolerated
Takes Actions Toward Purpose	• Gives examples of actions she has taken toward a career or job goal • Shows deliberate pursuit of a path or action • Indicates discovering desirable work through conscious choice	• Cannot give specific actions taken to arrive at or further a desired career path • Indicates a feeling of powerlessness over work and career • Describes a job that she dislikes, yet she is applying for a very similar position
Authenticity	• Gives examples of values conflicts and how he resolved them • Gives examples of steps he takes to builds trust with others • Gives examples of honoring commitments made to others	• Compromises values to fit into an organization or position • Is unable to give specific examples of steps taken to build trust • Reflects with little remorse or regret over commitments not made

(continued)

FIGURE 9.1 *Continued*

	PROS	CONS
	• Makes statements that match a sense of reality; statements in the interview seem to match and align; words and actions in the interview and in the behavioral examples are congruent	• Gives answers in the interview that do not align; inconsistencies in presentation, examples, and behaviors do not create a consistent picture of the candidate

Endnotes

1. Adele B. Lynn, *The EQ Difference* (New York: AMACOM, 2005).
2. Mihaly Csikszentmihalyi, *Flow: The Psychology of Optimal Experience* (New York: HarperCollins, 1990).
3. Thomas Sy, Susanna Tram, and Linda A. O'Hara, "Relation of Employee and Manager Emotional Intelligence to Job Satisfaction and Performance," *Journal of Vocational Behavior* 68, 3 (June 2006): 461.
4. Richard J. Leider, *Power of Purpose* (San Francisco: Berrett-Koehler Publishers, 1997).
5. "Upfront; Profits Get Personal," *New Zealand Management* (October 2005): 11.
6. Andrew N. Garman, Kristine D. Fitz, and Maria M. Fraser, "Communication and Relationship Management," *Journal of Healthcare Management* 51, 5 (September–October 2006): 291.
7. Ellen Galinsky, "The Changing Landscape of Work," *Generations* (Spring 2007): 7.
8. Nancy Gardner, "Should I Stay or Should I Go? What Makes Employees Voluntarily Leave or Keep Their Jobs," University of Washington Office of News and Information, August 6, 2007, http://uwnews.washington.edu/ni/article.asp?articleID=31234.
9. "Competence at Work Is a Function of Knowledge, Skill," *Businessline* (March 23, 2007): 1.
10. Adele Lynn, *In Search of Honor* (Belle Vernon, PA: BajonHouse, 1998).

CHAPTER 10

The EQ Fraud and Other Warning Signs

When considered as a whole, the employment process should paint an overall picture of the candidate. Neither the interview alone, nor certainly one question, should be used as the basis of hiring or rejecting a candidate. Rather, the interviewer or hiring manager should consider all facets of the employment process, from the initial resume and application to the final thank-you note (or lack of one).

Ultimately, the interviewer or hiring manager receives an overall impression, hopefully supported by facts uncovered during the process. Those facts come from a variety of sources, which could include the following: resume, reference checking, background checks, credential checking, testing, and the behavior-based interview. Each step uncovers clues or hints that serve to confirm or deny the candidate's suitability for the position. And each step is fraught with warning signs and cautions. For example, according to a survey by HireRight, an Internet company that checked out the resumes of more than two hundred thousand applicants, 80 percent of all resumes are misleading. The survey said that 20 percent listed fraudulent degrees, 30 percent altered employment dates, 40 percent inflated salaries, 30 percent contained inaccurate job descriptions, 25 percent said that they worked at companies that no longer exist, and 25 percent gave falsified references.[1] Other studies have indicated that anywhere from 25 to 40 percent of candidates have some misrepresentation or inaccuracy on their resumes.[2] Safe practice requires fact checking of some sort during the employment process. Employers can access many excellent sources that provide information on how to verify facts and check credentials. Employers also can hire reputable firms to provide verification services.

However, generally the interviewer or hiring manager sits in the only position to make judgments about what he hears and sees in the interview process. If you use a recruiting firm, that firm would serve as another layer of screening that could be helpful, but ultimately, the hiring manager determines whether the candidate will be offered the position. Therefore, navigating and interpreting interview responses requires a set of skills that includes listening for answers that indicate how the candidate will behave on the job based on his or her past behavior.

The first consideration in the interview is to look for trends or patterns. We've already said that one question shouldn't be the basis of rejecting or hiring a candidate. When interviewing a candidate, however, the interviewer should look for data that form a trend. Trends require the interviewer to take note. Trends can create a positive perception of the candidate's behavior or a negative perception of his behavior. Either way, spotting trends gives the interviewer useful information.

Trends worth considering include the following.

All One-Sided: Too Good to Be True

As you probably noted from the questions, the interview process seeks a balanced view of the candidate. The questions sometimes ask the candidate to elaborate on positive behaviors. At other times, the questions ask the candidate to discuss situations that didn't turn out so well. When planning the interview, be sure to select questions that ask for both viewpoints. Alternating between these types of questions allows the interviewer to gain a balanced and realistic view. Most people are not perfect, but nor are they completely flawed, so this process allows the candidate to reveal both strengths and weaknesses based on how he or she addressed real issues in the past. Just asking about positive behaviors or just seeking to uncover negative behaviors lacks the balanced viewpoint needed for proper assessment. One trend worth noting is whether or not the candidate discussed both positive and negative outcomes. If not, you may be left with the impression that the candidate has had only positive outcomes.

If the candidate discussed only or mostly positive outcomes and was unable or unwilling to give examples of how she addressed situations that didn't go so well, that should be of some concern. First, as the interviewer, you should examine your behavior. Did you provide an open forum? Did you explain to the candidate that you are interested in examples of how she behaved when things didn't go well? Did you encourage the candidate to give you examples? Did you give the candidate ample time to come up with examples? Did you preface or position your questions with an explanation of why you were asking about negative situations?

If you conducted the interview well, and the candidate was unable or unwilling to give examples of situations that didn't go so well, then the candidate may not be forthcoming. She has painted herself as too good to be true. Although every candidate wants to paint a positive picture during an interview, it's also critical that the candidate share information about her flaws. Emotionally intelligent people know that negative situations provide learning opportunities for future behavior. They can discuss how certain situations, especially ones where they didn't have a positive outcome, provided an opportunity to learn for future situations. People who are reluctant or unable to provide examples for the interviewer may either lack the self-awareness or be fearful of speaking about past situations that didn't go very well. Granted, it's difficult to come up with negative examples of our behavior, especially in a job interview, when we want to put our best foot forward. But most candidates can provide examples if given adequate time. A candidate who provides a balanced view demonstrates good self-awareness and courage.

Sometimes candidates clearly present a balanced view of situations. But they still sound too good to be true. Why? Because every negative situation they present somehow turned out to be a sudden epiphany of positive behavior change. Generally, negative situations help us understand our flaws and alert us to a need to change our behavior, but behavior change still requires effort. Emotionally intelligent people don't just suddenly change their behavior. They struggle with the same constraints as others. They may have a greater understanding and awareness of the impact of their behavior, but changing behavior still requires effort. While evaluating answers, listen for awareness, followed by repetitive efforts and struggles.

One candidate produced answers to each question aimed at uncovering flaws. After each example, he said, "I learned my lesson and never did that again." Another more realistic answer came from Mike, who said, "Those incidents helped me to understand my impact on others. Now I go into meetings watching and being more aware of my comments. Sometimes I still find that I blurt something out and must retract what I've said, but I'm much more aware and have definitely shown improvement." Although the first candidate may be very impressive because he claims that he instantly changes his behavior as a result of each situation, ask yourself, "Is that realistic?" An evaluation of these two candidates reveals that Mike's comments sound more realistic.

The following scenarios also signal concerns that the candidate may be "too good to be true" and warrant further investigation.

1. *The candidate's claims sound unrealistic based on her job title.* Although it is certainly possible for an entry-level clerk to make process improvements for her job or to make suggestions that can save money, it's probably unrealistic for someone with that title to launch a new line of products. This is especially a concern if the candidate makes several claims that don't add up.

2. *The candidate claims all the credit.* Sometimes a candidate speaks about accomplishments only in terms of self. This chorus of "I, I, I" and "me, me, me" fails to take into consideration the contributions of others. If a candidate describes an accomplishment, try to determine what he or she actually contributed. Is she claiming that she single-handedly accomplished it? Did others contribute? Ask directly about the role of others in the project. Also ask her to tell you exactly what she did.

3. *The candidate gives textbook answers.* When asking a candidate about conflict resolution, leadership, or other qualities, determine whether his answers sound like the latest management textbook; they may be just that. Press for details. The candidate should be able to tell you exactly what transpired. If not, he may be "creat-

ing" the situation as he goes along. The more details you ask, the greater the possibility that you'll get an accurate representation of the situation.

4. *The candidate always saves the day.* Listen carefully as the candidate describes his behavior. Does the candidate sound like a superman? If you begin to picture the candidate in blue tights with an *S* on his chest, consider that a warning sign. If nothing else, this behavior can rub teammates the wrong way. It can also indicate the candidate's need for attention. Remember, if you begin to form an impression, always dig for contrary evidence.

5. *The candidate has a charming personality.* Some candidates win over the interviewer with their charming manner. They create a conversation masterpiece because they have an easy-to-engage, witty, and warm manner—so much so, that the interviewer may actually be disarmed and forgo the details and diligence needed for proper interviewing standards. Now, don't misunderstand; we're not against charm. In some professions such as sales, charm is a useful tool that opens doors and makes people memorable. However, if the charm intentionally dismantles the interview process, then you may have been a victim of manipulation. A small percentage of people use charm as a negative tool. These highly skilled manipulators use charm to make their way in life. If you notice that the charm intensifies after you ask difficult questions, then consider that a warning sign. In particular, if the charm is followed by a deliberate attempt to sidetrack the conversation, then pay close attention. Two pieces of advice for the interviewer: First, stay the course and require the candidate to answer all questions. Stick to the questions that you've outlined. Besides being fair, the questions provide balance. Second, push or challenge the candidate on something. When challenged, master manipulators get angry. If you detect a flash of anger or irritation, continue to probe. Needless to say, anger or irritation in the interview foreshadows trouble down the road.

Remember, the behavior-based interview, when coupled with additional data accumulated from the resume, the employment check, the background check, and credential verification, gives an overall picture of the candidate. The dream candidate could be just that, but he could also be a fraud. Be sure to check carefully and empower yourself to pay attention to warning signs. A process that has more than one person interviewing candidates allows for checks and balances. Consensus during the interview process helps uncover possible frauds.

Other Behavior Trends

Spotting problematic behavior trends requires the interviewer or hiring manager to pay attention to the answers the candidates provide. Often, you'll detect patterns of blaming others, playing victim, being a know-it-all or other patterns that may not be desirable for your organization. It takes a combination of asking follow-up questions and knowing what these patterns sound like to avoid these kinds of hiring mistakes. When people demonstrate emotional intelligence, they act and reflect in a manner that takes responsibility for their behavior and the impact their behavior has on others. Let's examine how some common negative trends may sound during the interview process. Some of the common trends include the following:

1. *The candidate sounds like a victim.* The victim may be able to provide examples of situations that didn't turn out very well, but as he reflects on the incident during the explanation, you'll hear statements such as, "It really wasn't my fault" or "How was I supposed to know what to do?" You'll notice a pattern where the candidate lacks personal accountability to proactively solve problems or take actions. A very passive tone takes over—a learned helplessness, as described by Martin Seligman.[3] If you think about the job for which the candidate is interviewing, determine whether or not this type of thinking, which underlies victim behavior, would be a detriment. In most organizations, we have little tolerance for such behavior. You might think that this type of behavior occurs only at lower-level jobs; that simply is not true. I recently heard a CEO repeatedly explain issues within his organization using this tone.

2. *The candidate blames others.* Some people are able to justify just about any negative situation they find themselves in by blaming

others for their woes. During the interview process, the candidate may come up with examples of things that didn't turn out so well, but during the reflection and explanation, she will make statements such as "It wouldn't have turned out this way if Steve didn't . . ." or "Jan should have known that what he was asking me to do would create a problem" or "I never received any direction. I always had to figure things out for myself." Any of these statements can be true, but if during the course of the interview, you encounter numerous times when these types of statements appear, then that's cause for concern.

3. *The candidate sounds arrogant.* The interview process is a forum for candidates to discuss their skills and special talents. However, there is a distinction between demonstrating competence in an interview and sounding arrogant. When people explain situations or past behaviors with an arrogant tone, the perception they leave is one of superior importance. They communicate that they have rights over or are of greater value than others. Often these others are equals or subordinates. One candidate interviewing for a professional position repeatedly talked about the fact that she had better things to do with her time than clerical duties. When asked during the interview process about resolving conflict, she said that she would often remind people that "her work was not clerical in nature, and that would sometimes cause problems." The interviewer detected a hint of arrogance but wanted to pursue some facts. When the interviewer pressed for examples, he discovered that the candidate expected to dictate her e-mails to a clerical employee. That procedure is practically unheard-of today. She also explained that she didn't think it was her responsibility to obtain a file. If she needed a file for a particular client, she would tell others to get it for her.

4. *The candidate expresses much self-doubt.* Lack of confidence can spell disaster for some positions—especially leadership or sales positions. Listen for overall trends that point to a lack of confidence. It's important to distinguish between humility and lack of confidence. Someone who is humble may express a modest sense of his accomplishments, whereas someone who lacks confidence will express

doubt as to whether or not he can accomplish tasks. Again, look for trends. If someone continuously expresses doubt, then you may be hiring someone who is capable but may require much coaching to perform independently. That may be fine for some roles; for other roles, it may not be. Just be aware of the added commitment or coaching that may be required to get this person to perform.

5. *The candidate works as a lone wolf.* The interview should give you ample data to assess whether or not the candidate performs well as a team member. If the position requires performing as a team member, listen carefully for behaviors that indicate the candidate's preferences for working with others or working independently. When asked about past performance, listen for indications of when the candidate performs best. Because "teamwork" is a buzzword, many candidates may say they are team players. However, look for evidence, ask about preferences, and dig for examples that indicate that the person genuinely operates in a manner consistent with your organization's definition of teamwork.

6. *The candidate is overly concerned about power and authority figures.* We don't intend to minimize the importance of networks and social connections. In fact, we indicated earlier that these issues are part of emotional intelligence. However, with some candidates, as you listen carefully, you determine that the candidate relies more on power relationships and authority figures than on skills and competencies to get things accomplished. When asked about conflict resolution, one candidate for a senior director position continuously stated that he just went to one of the vice presidents who was his best friend and told him to fix the situation. Another candidate spoke of her mentor and used her mentor as a threat to others when things didn't go her way. These candidates obviously had strong relationships with people in power, but they failed to develop relationships and conflict-resolution skills with others. On the contrary, candidates who talk about what they learned from power or authority figures and how they used the information to be more effective with others portray a much different relationship with people in power.

7. *The candidate can't say "I don't know."* We've all been around a know-it-all. She has all the answers to all the questions all the time. It

would be very refreshing to hear this person say "I don't know." The interview process requires that the interviewer ask questions and the candidate answer them. However, the manner in which the candidate addresses the questions is very telling. If the candidate always puts herself into the role of authority or expert, that may indicate problems with others. Listen for the candidate's descriptions of interactions with coworkers and others. If she always has the answers and always tells others what to do or how something works, then she may be one of those people who just can't say "I don't know." "I don't know" invites others into the solution. If "I don't know" is coupled with, "What do you think?" others may even feel valued—especially if these words are spoken by a leader. When interviewing candidates for leadership positions, listen carefully. Do they see themselves as having the answers or as facilitators to come up with the answers? Even when leaders have the answers, facilitating others to come up with the answers broadens people's capabilities.

8. *The candidate demonstrates poor coping skills.* Sometimes during the interview, you gain important insight into the candidate's coping skills. Especially when you ask about conflict or difficult situations, the candidate may describe what she does to cope with problems. For example, when asked about conflicts with coworkers, one candidate said that she doesn't talk to the coworkers about the problems, but that she waits until she can return the insult. When the interviewer probed, the candidate described behaviors she used to intentionally set up coworkers for problems with customers. These kinds of coping skills set a destructive tone for the workplace. When asked about addressing problems at work, another candidate repeatedly said, "I don't get worked up about problems with others; I just head to the bar for a couple of martinis and forget about it." He repeated this at several points during the interview. If nothing else, it painted a rather flippant response to some sincere questions. Another candidate told the interviewer that she decided to job hunt because of conflict issues with coworkers. She revealed that she left a previous job for the same reasons. These behavior descriptions by the candidates demonstrate patterns of behavior. The interviewer must determine whether these behaviors constitute a trend of undesirable behavior.

9. *The candidate is angry.* Sometimes candidates demonstrate anger aimed at their former boss or company. And perhaps that anger is justified. However, in the interview process, anger is a warning sign. Most people try to put their best foot forward, so when anger seeps into the discussion, it raises a red flag. Anger can take many forms, including passive-aggressive forms such as sarcasm. When the candidate speaks about his present or previous employment, listen for the tone. If you detect a hint of anger, probe further. The questions in this book are designed to get even well-rehearsed candidates to reveal more of their behavior patterns than they normally would in an interview. By probing, you can further uncover unwanted behaviors. One interviewer determined that a candidate skirted questions about anger. When asked, "Tell me about a time when you were angry at work," he quickly diverted attention away from the question. The interviewer probed further and more directly. The candidate said that he did get angry on occasion but that it was not a problem. The interviewer continued to probe by asking the candidate to describe a specific incident when he got angry. The candidate said that he got angry at a staff meeting when he was being blamed for market performance. The interviewer continued to probe and asked, "What did you do and say at this meeting when you were being blamed for market performance?" The interviewer could see that the candidate was getting angry. He said in a dismissive way, "I don't see why this is relevant to this interview." This candidate's reluctance to speak openly about the situation, compounded by his dismissive comment, caused the interviewer concern about the candidate's behavior related to anger.

10. *The candidate is a skeptic or a cynic.* Many professions train people in critical-thinking skills. Critical-thinking skills in engineers, accountants, and others make for good decisions and sound practices. After all, we don't want people to assume that the bridge trusses will hold; we want them to be sure. In fact, the more skeptical, the better. It causes people to check and double- check to ensure the facts. However, when this thinking is applied to everything else in the organization, it can create an atmosphere of distrust. Ideally, we want to hire candidates who separate the critical thinking required on technical projects or disciplines from the skepticism or critical

thinking aimed toward coworkers, management, or the organization. However, being a team player and a good follower often requires a leap of faith. Faith in the mission, faith in the performance of others, faith in the leader, and faith in the organization's motives result in a set of behaviors quite different from those of an employee who lacks such belief. Such faith doesn't prohibit people from speaking up, but the manner in which they speak up is often different if cynicism rules. Cynical employees question everything. They don't believe in the organization, its mission, or their coworkers. This constant questioning can be tiring and can take valuable resources away from accomplishing goals. During the interview process, listen for this quality. When the candidate describes his behavior, does he recount constant questioning and cynicism? Does he describe situations where he is always skeptical of a coworker's skills or performance? Does he describe situations when he constantly questions the organization's direction or mission? Don't forget; we're looking for trends and the manner in which people express themselves. Expressing contrary opinions isn't a negative quality. Contrary opinions expressed with heavy doses of cynicism and skepticism create a negative work climate and may not be in your organization's best interest.

A Word About Instinct

If a new hire doesn't work out, you'll often hear the comment "Something told me this wasn't going to work." Indeed, experienced interviewers and hiring managers often do have instincts that lead them to certain conclusions about a candidate. In fact, in a study conducted at the University of Toledo, after viewing a fifteen-second clip of an applicant initially meeting and shaking hands with the interviewer, strangers were able to predict the outcome of the interview on nine of the eleven traits that the applicant was being judged on.[4] Instinct proved to be accurate on most of the traits. In another case, a research team at the University of Texas tested three thousand managers and found that top executives rated significantly higher in intuition tests than middle- or lower-level managers. They relied on intuition in decision making, especially when there was uncertainty or limited or unclear facts.[5] If that's the case, why bother interviewing at all? Let's just have some highly intuitive people watch fifteen-second video clips. No, we're not advocating abandoning good interviewing practice, data checking, and other methods that verify facts in favor of instinct. However, instinct does play a role in the process.

We suggest that you carefully plan and execute the interview process, but as you're summing up your experience with the candidate, pay attention to the overall impression, or instinct, that you have about the candidate. Before the interview ends, ask yourself for this information; then use your instinct as a signal to pursue more data. Maybe you would like to verify a feeling that you have about the person's openness or candidness. Perhaps you have some lingering feeling about whether the candidate is a team player. Or maybe there's some concern that the candidate may be slightly arrogant. Use this instinct to probe further. Add some questions that give you a second look. Or perhaps review the questions that led you to this impression and probe further to clarify the candidate's behavior pattern. Your objective is not to verify your feeling, but to objectively gain a second view of the candidate. You may find that you misinterpreted something the candidate said, or you could find that your impression was accurate. Either way, the interview process allows you to gain information that you can't gain by looking at a resume. Use your time to look deeply at the behavior patterns the candidate presents. As you empower that overall feeling or impression and ask questions aimed at discovering new information about the candidate's behavior patterns, you receive a balanced view of the candidate's strengths and weaknesses. No candidate is without flaws. The interview process simply allows flaws and strengths to surface so you can determine the best fit for the job and the organization.

Endnotes

1. J.F. Tamen, "Job Applicants' Resumes Are Often Riddled with Misinformation," *Knight Ridder Tribune Business News* (February 2003).
2. Ibid.
3. Martin Seligman, *Learned Optimism* (New York: Simon and Schuster, 1998).
4. Lucia Cockroft, "Basic Instinct," *Personnel Today,* February 21, 2006.
5. W. Agor, *The Logic of Intuitive Decision Making* (Austin: University of Texas Press, 2006).

CHAPTER 11

A Final Word

Hiring the right person for the job remains a critically important task in our organizations. The cost of a bad decision remains high, both in terms of wasted time and resources and in terms of risk. Also, the sheer volume of hiring to replace the aging workforce continues to rise, thus creating a competitive climate for finding talent. These trends continue to cause employers to use all the resources possible to find the best person for the job and the organization.

Resources that help in the decision making process include a variety of fact checking, resume verification, background checks, testing, and the behavior-based interview. All these resources play a role in the employment process. However, the interview remains the face-to-face encounter where impressions are verified, conclusions are drawn, and decisions rest. Interviewing for emotional intelligence adds another dimension to the decision-making process. It expands the behavior-based interview to allow the interviewer or hiring manager to see a more detailed picture of the candidate. It also encourages the candidate to reveal important information about his thought patterns, which lead to behaviors in the workplace.

As organizations become more sophisticated in understanding the competencies that lead to success, they will place an increased emphasis on interviewing for emotional intelligence. We no longer linger in darkness about the factors that lead to high performance. The body of research linking emotional intelligence to job performance crosses job duties, organization types, and industries. We continue to find evidence that the best performers in our organizations are technically competent individuals with important elements of emotional intelligence. Functional or technical competence will always be important, but as we compete in different markets, interact with culturally different clients and customers, manage foreign workforces, and interact with people of all types, those most skilled in managing themselves and their interactions with others will prove to be invaluable.

When you hire people who demonstrate emotional intelligence, you build an organization that can function, not just today, but also tomorrow. Emotionally intelligent people possess the skill of reading different environments and then adjusting or adapting their behavior to deliver the best results. People without this skill rely solely on past successful behavior. However, if the environment changes, and it surely will, their past behavior may not fit future situations. An example of this occurs when a successful manager is promoted to a cross-functional director-level position. Perhaps part of the manager's past success was grounded in his hands-on approach. At a cross-functional director level, that hands-on approach may prove detrimental. Emotional intelligence enables that new director to understand that his past approach was suited to his past position, but not to his new position. The new director's ability to read the different environment his new title demands saves him the pain of performing at a level that was once appropriate but no longer delivers results. In fact, if the director continued to function at that past level, he may even fail because his relationships with peers require a different set of behaviors. A similar situation occurs when a manager transitions to a new team, an international assignment, or a new company. Is that manager able to read the environment and understand the set of behaviors that will produce results in this new assignment? Can he read the environment in the moment and behave in a manner that will produce the best results? As you craft interview questions aimed at the emotional intelligence competencies required for each position, you'll be able to predict with greater accuracy whether or not a candidate will succeed, and you'll build an organization equipped for the future.

Hiring emotionally intelligent employees gives organizations another huge advantage. Great organizational cultures consist of highly emotionally intelligent people. As you hire emotionally intelligent people to work in your company or organization, you change the essence of the interactions within the culture. Emotionally intelligent people don't scream and yell; they don't belittle peers. Instead, they build solid, genuine relationships, they resolve conflict in a healthy manner, they listen, and they have the courage to speak the truth in a constructive way. These qualities serve as a magnet for recruiting new hires. Who wouldn't want to work for a company whose people demonstrate these types of behaviors? As the market for talent grows tighter, by adjusting your hiring practices to screen for emotional intelligence, you build a solid foundation on which recruiting new hires becomes easier due to the culture of excellence you create.

Not only does recruitment become easier, but retention improves. Numerous studies link job satisfaction, retention, and organizational culture. Today's talent isn't willing to stay in a company that doesn't deliver job satisfaction. The competitive talent market allows candidates the luxury of picking and choosing not only where they want to work, but whether or not they want to remain there. We've already established the high cost of turnover, so by changing your hiring practices, you create a culture where people are not only attracted to your organization, but also choose to remain.

If your organization purports to have an organizational culture that values people or declares workplace values such as respect or teamwork or trust or customer satisfaction, then the best way to ensure that these qualities are met is to hire technically functional people who behave in a manner that is consistent with these intentions. Interviewing for emotional intelligence gives the hiring manager or interviewer a much closer look at whether or not a candidate's behaviors will deliver these results.

APPENDIX 1

Emotional Intelligence
Table of Competencies

AREA OF EMOTIONAL INTELLIGENCE	DEFINITION	COMPETENCIES
Self-Awareness and Self-Control	The ability to fully understand oneself and one's impact on others and to use that information to manage oneself productively	*Self-Awareness* • Impact on others: An accurate understanding of how one's behavior or words affect others • Emotional and inner awareness: An accurate understanding of how one's emotions and thoughts affect behaviors • Accurate self-assessment: An honest assessment of strengths and weaknesses *Self-Control* • Emotional expression: The ability to manage anger, stress, excitement, and frustration

AREA OF EMOTIONAL INTELLIGENCE	DEFINITION	COMPETENCIES
		• Courage: The ability to manage fear • Resilience: The ability to manage disappoint-ment or failure
Empathy	Ability to understand the perspective of others	• Respectful listening: Listening respectfully to others to develop a deep understanding of others' points of view • Feeling the impact on others: The ability to assess and determine how situations as well as one's words and actions affect others • Service orientation: The desire to help others
Social Expertness	Ability to build genuine relationships and bonds and express caring, concern, and conflict in healthy ways	• Building relationships: The ability to build social bonds • Collaboration: The ability to invite others in and value their thoughts related to ideas, projects, and work • Conflict resolution: The ability to resolve differences • Organizational savvy: The ability to under-stand and maneuver within organizations

AREA OF EMOTIONAL INTELLIGENCE	DEFINITION	COMPETENCIES
Personal Influence	Ability to positively lead and inspire others as well as oneself	*Influencing Others* • Leading others: The ability to have others follow you • Creating a positive work climate: The ability to create an inspiring culture • Getting results through others: The ability to achieve goals through others *Influencing Self* • Self-confidence: An appropriate belief in one's skills or abilities • Initiative and accountability: Being internally guided to take steps or actions and taking responsibility for those actions • Goal orientation: Setting goals for oneself and living and working toward goals • Optimism: Having a tendency to look at the bright side of things and to be hopeful for the best • Flexibility: The ability to adapt and bend to the needs of others or situations as appropriate

AREA OF EMOTIONAL INTELLIGENCE	DEFINITION	COMPETENCIES
Mastery of Purpose and Vision	Ability to bring authenticity to one's life and live out one's intentions and values	• Understanding one's purpose and values: Having a clearly defined purpose and values • Taking actions toward one's purpose: Taking actions to advance one's purpose • Authenticity: Alignment and transparency of one's motives, actions, intentions, values, and purpose

APPENDIX 2

Questions by Area and Competencies

Self-Awareness	
Impact on Others	• Tell me about a time when you did or said something and it had a positive impact on a coworker, a customer, or an employee.
	• Tell me about a time when you did or said something and it had a negative impact on a coworker, a customer, or an employee.
	• Tell me about a time when you were surprised about the positive impact your behavior or words had on a coworker, a customer, or an employee. How did you learn this information? What did you do when you learned this information?
	• Tell me about a time when you were surprised about the negative impact your behavior or words had on a coworker, a customer, or an employee. How did you learn this information? What did you do when you learned this information?
	• Describe a time when you knew you did or said something that caused a problem for a coworker, a customer, or an employee. How did you know it caused a problem?

- Can you think of a time when someone interpreted something you said or did in a negative way, even though you didn't intend for it to be negative? Tell me about that.

- How do you know if your words or behaviors have a positive impact on others?

- How do you know if your words or behaviors have a negative impact on others?

- Have you ever noticed that someone at work was having a bad day? How did you know? What did you do?

- Have you ever decided to delay presenting an idea to someone at work because the timing wasn't right? What did you base that decision on? What did you do?

- Have you ever noticed that you were annoying someone at work? What did you base that on? What did you do?

- Have you ever been in a situation where you thought you needed to adjust or modify your behavior? How did you know?

Emotional and Inner Awareness

- Tell me about a time when you were distracted or preoccupied about something. How did you know? What impact did that have on your performance? What impact did it have on others at work?

- Tell me about a time when you were in a good mood at work. How did that affect your performance? What impact did your mood have on others at work?

- Describe a time when you were angry about something at work. How did that affect your performance? What impact did it have on others at work?

- Tell me about a time when the mood or attitude of your coworkers, employees, or others affected you.

- Describe a time when you were aware that your mood was affecting how you were behaving at work.

- Tell me about some situations or people that annoy you in your present (or previous) position. Tell me what you do about these situations or people.

- Tell me about a time when you were able to avoid a negative situation at work. How did you know it was going to be negative? Tell me what you did.

- Describe some situations or circumstances that bring out your best at work. How do you behave during those times?

- Describe some situations or circumstances that bring out your worst at work. How do you behave during those times? What do you do about those times?

- Tell me about a time when you purposely prepared yourself to deal with a situation that you knew would be negative. What did you do? How did it work out?

- Tell me about a time when something that you had responsibility for at work didn't go well. Who's fault was it? (This is a leading question—it's assuming blame. The candidate should consider his or her own role in the problem.)

- Tell me about a time at work when others didn't cooperate with you. How would you analyze that situation?

- Tell me about a conflict you had at work. How would you analyze that conflict?

- Have you ever unintentionally insulted or offended someone at work? How did you handle that?

- Tell me about a time when you reacted to something or someone in the workplace in a way that was not aligned with your intentions. What did you do after this situation?

Accurate Self-Assessment
- Describe a time when you received feedback about your performance and were in agreement. What did you agree with?

- Describe a time when you received feedback about your performance and you disagreed with that feedback. What did you disagree with?

- Was there ever a time when you initially disagreed with feedback you received and later came to accept it? Tell me about that.

- Were you ever surprised by criticism you received? What was the criticism and why were you surprised?

- What has been a consistent strength of yours? What evidence do you have that this is an area in which you are strong?

- What has been a consistent area of development for you? How do you know that this is an area of development for you?

- List three things you have learned about yourself in the last year that are relevant to the way you work. How did you learn this information? Describe a time when you used this new information.

Self-Control or Self-Management

Emotional Expression

- Describe some things that make you angry or frustrated at work. Tell me what you do in those situations.

- Describe some types of situations where you are likely to get annoyed at work. What do you do when you get annoyed?

- Tell me about a time when you were angry with someone at work. What did you do?

- Has there ever been a situation at work where you said something and later regretted saying it? Tell me about that.

- Tell me about a time when you lost your temper at work. What did you do? What result did this have?

- Tell me about a time when you had too much to do at work and it was causing you to feel stressed. What did you do?

- What do you do when you are feeling stressed at work?

- Describe a stressful situation at work. What do you do?

- Describe a situation at work when you were very enthusiastic about something. How did your enthusiasm affect others?

- Describe a time when you felt excited about work.

- When do you look forward to going to work?

- Was there ever a time at work when you had to temper your enthusiasm for something?

- Describe a time when you felt grateful at work. What did you do?

- Give me an example of when you expressed gratitude toward someone at work.

Courage or Assertiveness

- Tell me about a time when you spoke up about something in the workplace. What was the issue? Why did you speak up about it? What did you say? What did others think?

- Has there ever been a situation at work where you wish you had said something in a meeting or encounter but didn't? Tell me about that.

- Describe what you did the last time someone blamed you for something at work that wasn't your fault. What did you do?

- Describe a time when you were right and you knew you were right, but the other party (customer, coworker, your boss) at work didn't believe you. What did you do?

- Tell me about a time when you felt something was unfair at work. What did you do?

- Tell me about a time when you knew that you were told to do something that you thought wasn't a good idea. What did you do?

For managers or leaders:

- Tell me about a time when you disagreed about the direction of the company or a policy. What did you do?
- Describe a time when you and a peer were at odds about a particular decision or direction. What did you do?
- Tell me about a time when your boss had a particular opinion that differed from yours. What did you do?
- Tell me about a time when you disagreed with a goal that you were told to achieve. How did that go?
- Describe a difficult performance discussion that you had with an employee.
- Tell me about a time when you decided not to discuss an issue with an employee. What did you consider?

Resilience

- Tell me about a time when you felt that you were defeated at work. What did you do?
- Tell me about a time when you were distracted or preoccupied about something. What did you do?
- Tell me about a time when you felt like giving up on something. What did you do?
- Describe a time when you didn't think things could get any worse, and then they did. What did you do?
- Tell me about a time when you decided to give up on a goal.
- Tell me about a time when you were overwhelmed at your last job. How often does that occur? What do you do about it?
- Talk about the last time you were criticized at work. How did that go?

Awareness in the Moment	• Tell me about a time when you realized that a conversation wasn't going very well. (Is the candidate able to realize during the situation the dynamics of the situation?) What did you do? (Is the candidate able to redirect the conversation for a better outcome?)
	• Tell me about a time when you realized that you weren't speaking up during a meeting. What did you do?
	• Tell me about a time when you realized that something was best left unsaid. What did you do?
Planning Tone	• Tell me about a time when you deliberately planned the tone of a particular conversation. (This indicates that the candidate is aware that tone affects outcome.) How did you do that? (This indicates skill.) What result did it have?
	• In your present job, can you tell me about some situations when you must think about how you are going to say something before saying it? What must you consider?
	• Tell me about a time when you planned the way you phrased a problem or situation so that you could get the best result.
	• Tell me about a time when you missed an opportunity to set the tone in a discussion. What happened?

Empathy

Respectful Listening	• Think about a time when you didn't understand something in the workplace. What did you do?
	• Describe a situation when you didn't understand why someone was acting a certain way or taking a certain position on some issue? What did you do?

- Describe a time when you jumped to conclusions.

- Tell me about a conversation with a coworker, employee, or customer that didn't go very well. What specifically occurred?

For managers or leaders:

- Tell me about a time when you learned something by listening to an employee.

- Describe a time when you asked someone for information about a problem.

Feeling the Impact on Others

- Tell me about a situation when you sensed something was bothering a peer or coworker. How did you know? What did you do?

- Describe a situation when you knew that something was wrong with a relationship you had with a peer, customer, or supervisor. What did you do?

- Relate a situation in which you determined that something that you did or said didn't go over very well. How did you know?

- Describe a time when you said something or did something that had a negative effect on someone.

- Describe a time when you did or said something that had a negative effect on someone and you were unaware of it until someone else brought it to your attention.

For managers or leaders:

- Tell me about a time when you sensed that an employee was struggling. How did you know? What did you do?

- Tell me about a time when you noticed that your staff was overwhelmed. How did you know? What did you do?

- Describe a time when a change you were implementing caused stress for your staff. How did you know? What did you do?

Service Orientation

- Tell me about a time when you offered assistance to someone without being asked. What did you do?

- Describe a situation when you offered assistance to someone even though it was outside of your job description. What did you do?

- Relate an instance when someone needed help and you couldn't help him. What did you do?

- Tell me about a time when you recognized that someone needed help. What did you do?

- Describe a situation when you were asked to help someone at work. What did you think about that?

- Was there ever a time when you resented helping someone at work? Tell me about that.

For the manager or leader:

- Tell me about a time when an employee was struggling. What did you do?

Social Expertness

Building Relationships

- Who are some key people within your organization who you currently must work with on a regular basis to get your work done? Describe your relationship with these people.

- Describe your present responsibility for building and maintaining relationships at work. Whom do you build relationships with? How? Why?

- Tell me about a time when you were able to get something done at work because of a relationship you had with another person.

- Tell me about some of the people whom you have to work with on a regular basis that you find difficult to get along with. What have you done to build stronger relationships with these people?

- Tell me about a situation when you "won someone over" at work. What did you do?

- Tell me about someone who is resistant to you. What did you do?

- Tell me about your relationship with your manager. What works well? What would you like to see improved?

- What do you do that makes you a good follower?

Collaboration

- Tell me how you recently solved a work problem. What process did you use?

- Describe a time when you had to solve a problem that involved or affected other people within the company. How did you solve it?

- Have you ever implemented an idea or solved a problem and had your solution meet with resistance? What do you think you could have done to avoid the resistance?

- Describe a time when you sought someone's ideas or opinions about a project or idea you were working on.

- Was there ever a time when you rejected someone's idea or opinion about a project? Tell me about that?

- Tell me about a time when you offered your idea or opinion to someone.

- Describe a time when your input improved someone's work.

- Have you ever offered an idea or opinion at work and had nothing to gain from it? Tell me about that.

Conflict Resolution	• Tell me about a dispute with a peer. What was it about? What did you do? How did it end up?
	• Tell me about a time when someone suggested something that you disagreed with. What did you say?
	• How have you resolved differences with peers or others? Tell me about the process you use to resolve your differences.
	• Have you ever encountered someone at work who was unreasonable? What did you do?

For managers or leaders:

• Tell me about a time when there was a dispute between two coworkers. What did you do?

• Tell me about a time when you had a conflict with an employee. What did you do? How was it resolved?

• Describe a time when someone felt that you were unfair. What did you do?

• Relate an incident when someone verbally attacked you about something you said or did. What did you do?

Organizational Savvy	• Did you ever have an opportunity to advance a new idea at your last job? How did you go about doing that?
	• Tell me about a time when you gained support for an idea that you had. How did you do that? Why was this idea important to you?
	• Describe a time when you couldn't get support for an idea that you had. What happened? Why was this idea important to you?
	• Within your present position, what happens when you run into someone who isn't supporting your efforts to get things done? Describe what you do.

- Have you ever had someone undermine your efforts? What did you do?

- How can you tell who makes decisions in your organization?

- Tell me about a time when you needed support from peers in order to get an idea across. How did you gain that support? Why was it important to you to get that particular idea or initiative accomplished?

Personal Influence—Influencing Self

Self-Confidence
- Tell me about a time when you took on a task that you considered "out of your comfort zone." How did you feel? Why did you do it? Did you think you were going to succeed or fail?

- If you were going to try to persuade me regarding something, how would you do it?

- Describe a time when you interjected a different point of view or a different side of an issue. How did you go about doing that?

- Tell me about a time when you were confident enough to disagree with something or someone.

- Tell me about your strengths. How do you know they are your strengths? How do you measure your strengths? What feedback have you gotten that indicates that this quality is a strength?

- Tell me about a time that you were concerned about being successful at a task or you thought you were going to fail. What did you do?

- When do you typically ask for assistance? Describe the last time you asked for help on something.

- How do you think you're going to perform at this job?

For managers and leaders:

- Tell me about a time when you had to implement a change. What did you say to your staff? How did you convince them to follow you?

- Tell me about a time when you had to lead others in a certain direction and you had some doubts. What did you do? What did you say?

- Have you ever experienced a time when others questioned your ability to lead? Tell me about that. What did you do?

Initiative and Accountability

- Tell me about a time when you decided on your own that something needed to be done. What did you do?

- Describe a time when you did more than was required on your job. How did you feel about that?

- Have you ever made any improvements to your work without being asked? Give me some examples. How did you do it?

- When you perform your present job, have you ever thought about a way to improve the quality of the product or service that you provide? Tell me about that.

- Have you ever come up with a way to cut costs in your present position? What did that entail? How did you go about doing it?

- Have you ever thought of a way to perform your present job in less time? What did you do about it?

- Tell me about a time when something you did resulted in a change for your department or area. How did you go about doing it? How did you feel about that?

- Have you ever taken the initiative to do something that didn't work out? Describe that situation. What did you do? How did you feel about that?

- Have you ever solved a work-related problem that had been a problem for a long time? What did you do? How did you do it?

- Have you ever taken an action and gotten blamed when it didn't work out? Describe what happened.

Goal Orientation

- Describe some goals for your present position. How were these goals determined? Do you meet these goals on a regular basis?

- Have you ever thought that these goals were unrealistic? Why?

- Have you ever had a goal at work that you didn't meet? How did you feel about that?

- Tell me about a goal that you imposed on yourself at work. Why did you decide on that particular goal?

- Tell me about a time when you didn't achieve something that you set out to do. What happened? How did you feel about that?

- What goals do you have right now?

- What goals did you accomplish last year?

- Tell me about a time when you didn't feel like working. What did you do?

- Describe your process for setting goals for yourself.

For the manager or leader:

- How do you set goals for those who report to you? Describe the process you use to set goals within your unit or department.

- How have you helped others set goals?

- How do you ensure that the goals are aligned with the business strategy?

- Tell me about a time when someone who reported to you did not reach an important goal. What did you do?

Optimism	• Tell me about a project that you knew was not going to deliver results. How did you know?
	• Describe a time when you tried something new at work. How did that work? Would you do it again? Why or why not?
	• Describe a situation at work when you were optimistic and it affected the outcome.
	• Describe a situation at work when others wanted to move forward on something and you didn't think it was a good idea. Why didn't you think it would work? What did you do?
	• Describe a time when you were more optimistic than others at work about a particular project. What did you do?
	• Tell me about a time when you had misplaced optimism. How did you proceed?
	• Tell me about a time when you didn't believe that a project was going to turn out on time, on budget, or on track. Why did you think it was going to be a problem?
	• Give me a situation where you believed that something was going to be successful and it was. How did you know?
	• Tell me about a time when someone on your team was negative about an outcome. How did it affect you?
Flexibility	• Describe a time when you had to change your plans to accommodate someone else at work. How did you feel about that?
	• Tell me about a time when something at work was changing. How have you adapted to the change? How did you feel about the change?
	• Relate a time when you wanted something at work to remain the same, but others didn't. What did you do? How did you feel about that?

- Describe a time when you had to learn something new. How did you feel about that? How have you adapted to the new system?

- Tell me about a time when you had trouble adjusting to a change. What did you find difficult?

- Give me an example of a time when you were flexible.

- Give me an example of a time when you weren't very flexible.

- Tell me about a time when you had to reconsider how to interact or behave because you weren't getting the results you required.

- Were there any behaviors that you had to abandon that worked for you in a previous job that didn't work in a new job? How did you know these behaviors didn't or wouldn't work in your new job?

For managers or leaders:

- Tell me about a time as a manager that you found it necessary to bend the rules. What did you do? Why did you do it? How did you feel about it?

- Tell me about a time when you were flexible and accommodated the needs of someone on your staff. How did you feel about that?

- As a manager, have you ever been flexible and later regretted it?

- What types of behaviors did you need to develop when you transitioned from worker to supervisor? From manager to director?

- Were there any behaviors that you had to abandon that worked for you in a previous role that didn't work in a new role? How did you know these behaviors didn't or wouldn't work in your new role?

- Was there ever a time when you changed roles or jobs or organizations that you had to let go of behaviors that contributed to your success in past situations?

Personal Influence—Influencing Others

Leading Others

- Tell me about a time you had an idea and you got other people to follow you. What did you do?

- Describe a time when others relied on you and followed your lead.

- Tell me about a time when you were able to influence others. How did you do it? How did you feel about influencing others?

- Describe a time when you took charge of a situation.

- Tell me about a time when others looked to you for direction. What did you do? How did you feel about that?

For managers and leaders:

- How do you get people to follow you? What do you do? How do you influence them?

- Tell me about a time when someone was resisting you. What did you do?

- Describe a time when you were able to get people to follow you on a controversial issue.

- Tell me about a time when you united your followers around an issue.

- Describe a time when you influenced people to follow you when you did not have positional authority.

- Give me an example of when you influenced your peers.

- Give me an example of when you influenced your boss.

Creating a Positive Culture

For leaders and managers:

- Describe the climate or culture of your present department.

- What specific steps do you take to set the tone within your department?

- How is the climate within your department different from that of other areas within your company?
- What evidence do you have that you've created a positive climate or culture?
- Describe the ideal climate of a department. What actions do you think a leader must take to create an ideal climate?
- Tell me about a time when your staff was not very energized. What did you do?
- Tell me about a time when someone expressed concerns about the working climate of your department. What did you do?
- Describe a situation when an employee was disrupting the climate you were trying to establish. What did you do?

For employees:
- Describe a positive working climate. What would it feel like? What do you do to create a positive working climate every day?
- Give me some examples of what you do to ensure that your coworkers have a positive day.
- Give me an example of some actions you've taken with a negative coworker. What have you done to create a more positive working relationship with this person?
- How do you support your supervisor in creating a positive climate in your work unit?

Getting Results Through Others

For managers or leaders:
- Describe some of the results you've achieved in your area within the past year. How did you achieve those results?
- In what areas did you fall short of delivering the results you wanted to deliver? Why did you fall short? What could you have done differently?

- Describe how you typically get results from other people.

- Tell me how you set goals for your staff. Give me an example of a time when someone wasn't meeting a goal. What did you do?

- Has there ever been a time when no matter what you did, someone was unable to reach a goal? What did you do?

- What have you done to share your expectations with your department?

- Have you ever set a goal too low? What did you do?

- Tell me about a time when someone was resisting you, your ideas, or your authority. What did you do?

- Tell me about a time that you were wrong in the way that you addressed an employee situation.

- As a manager, tell me about a time when you didn't have enough resources to do the job. What did you do?

For employees:

- Describe a situation when your actions helped others achieve results or goals.

Mastery of Purpose and Vision

Understanding Purpose and Values

- Describe a time when you were lost in your work in a good way—when time just flew by and you were totally absorbed in what you were doing.

- Tell me about a time when you felt bored at work.

- Describe your ideal job.

- Describe the worst possible job for you.

- What type of work would you find most inspiring?

Takes Actions Toward Purpose	• How did you decide on your chosen field of endeavor, college major, or line of work? What influenced you? What actions did you take to end up in this field?
	• What do you like about your chosen field? What do you dislike?
	• What actions have you taken related to your career that you were pleased you took? What pleases you about your actions?
	• Have you ever pursued a career-related goal, perhaps a credential or a specific job, only to discover that when you achieved your goal you were disappointed? Tell me about that.
Authenticity	• Describe a situation where you found yourself in a values conflict. What did you do?
	• Tell me about a situation at work where you felt that you had to compromise your beliefs or values.
	• Describe a time when you felt very strongly about something that happened at work—something you considered to be an affront to your values. What did you do?
	• Tell me how you gain people's trust. What do you do? What actions did you take?
	• Tell me about a time when you lost someone's trust.
	• Describe how you know you have honored your commitments that you've made to others.
	• Tell me about a time when you failed to honor a commitment.
	• Has there ever been a time when you promised something at work and were unable to deliver it? How did you feel about that?
	• Tell me about a time when you did less than your fair share at work or you got out of a difficult assignment. How did you feel about that?

INDEX

Accountability, 86. *See also* Initiative, as personal influence competency
Action, as outcome of purpose and vision, 133–135, 139
Adaptability. *See* Flexibility and adaptability
Aggression, expression in the workplace, 35
Anger, 21, 36–39, 150
Anxiety, as self-defeating emotion, 21
Arrogance, 147
Assertiveness. *See* Courage/assertiveness
Attitude, positive, 99
Authenticity, 130
  assessment of, 135–140, 160, 180
  examples of, 136–137
  as purpose and vision competency, 14, 135–140, 160
Authority, 115, 116, 121–122. *See also* Leaders; Leadership
Authority figures, over reliance on, 148

Baby boomer generation, 1–2
Background checks, on job applicants, 141–142, 145–146
Behavior, 102–103, 146–151
Belief systems, violations of, 136
Bell Laboratories, 78
Bergquist, W.H., 102
Blaming, of others, 146–147
Body language, relationship to self-confidence, 87, 89i
Bullying, 35

Cadbury Schweppes, 86
Center for Creative Leadership, 66
Change, flexibility associated with, 101–102, 105–106
Christ, 112
Collaboration, 10, 12–13, 71–74, 82, 98, 124, 158, 170
Commitment(s). 2, 71, 135–136
Communication
  face-to-face, in conflict resolution, 75
  in performance management, 124
  physician-patient, 17
  planning the tome of conversations, 47–49
Compassion, 56, 651–62
Confidence. *See* Self-confidence, as personal influence competency

Conflict, sources of, 74
Conflict resolution, 10, 13, 45–46, 66, 74–78, 82, 149–150, 158, 171
Confrontation, avoidance of, 39–40
Conscientiousness, 2
Conversations, planning the tone of, 47–49, 167
Coping skills, poor, 149–150
Courage/assertiveness, as self-management competency, 12, 39–42
  assessment of, 40–42, 49, 158–161
Csikszentmihalyi, Mihaly, 130–131
Culture, of the workplace. *See* Work climate
Cynicism, 150–151

Deceit, 138
Decision making, mastery of purpose and vision in, 130
Deming, W. Edwards, 113
Depression, as self-defeating emotion, 21
Discipline, progressive, 125
Downsizing, 43
Doyle, Richard, 86

EI. *See* Emotional intelligence
Emotion(s), 21, 129–130
Emotional expression, as self-control competency, 12, 34, 35–39
  assessment of, 36–39, 49, 164–167
  examples of, 35–36
  positive, 38
Emotional intelligence
  differentiated from social skills, 7–8
  model of, 8–14. *See also* Empathy; Mastery of purpose and vision; Personal influence; Self-control; Social awareness; Social expertness
Emotional intelligence competencies. *See* Empathy; Mastery of purpose and vision; Personal influence; Self-control; Social awareness; Social expertness
Emotional intelligence interviews, 3–5, 145–146. *See also* Questions and answers, in emotional intelligence interviews
Empathy, 8, 12, 53–64, 158
  competencies associated with, 12

Empathy (*continued*)
    feeling the impact on others, 54, 56–58, 62, 158, 168–171
    respectful listening, 54–56, 62, 158, 167–170
    service orientation, 54, 58–62, 63, 158, 169
  components of, 12
  as internal function, 9–10
Employees, 1–2
  relationship with bosses/supervisors, 70–71
  responsibility for a positive work climate, 120–121
Employee turnover, 2, 3, 68
Employment interviews, 142
EQ Difference (Lynn), 130

Failure, 43, 66
Fear, 35, 36, 39–40
Flexibility and adaptability, as personal influence competencies, 14, 86, 159
  assessment of, 101–107
"Flow," in work, 130–131, 132
Follower skills, 71
Fraudulent information, on resumes, 141–142

Goal achievement/orientation, as personal influence competency, 13, 14, 86, 94–98, 108, 159
  assessment of, 94–98, 108, 121–127, 174
  collaboration in, 98, 124
  differentiated from initiative, 95
  examples of, 95–96, 122
  relationship to resilience, 43
  resistance to, 124–125
  short-term or long-term, 97
Goals, conflicted, 136

Harassment, expression in the workplace, 35
Hay Group, 95
"Headhunters," executive, 68
Helpfulness. *See* Service orientation
HireRight, 141
Hospitality, "emotional," 59
Hostility, as self-defeating emotion, 21
Humility, 147–148

Impact on others, 11, 16–20, 29. *See also* Personal influence
  assessment of, 18–20, 161–164, 168–171
  empathy and, 54, 56–58, 62, 168–171
  examples of, 16–18
Influence. *See* Personal influence
Initiative, as personal influence competency, 13, 86, 91–94, 107, 159
  assessment of, 91–94, 107, 173–176
  differentiated from goal orientation, 95
  examples of, 91–92
Instinct, in decision making, 151–152
Interviewers, instinct-based decision making ability of, 151–152
Interviews. *See* Emotional intelligence interviews
"In the moment" awareness, 45–47, 167

Job dissatisfaction/satisfaction, 2, 130–133

Kelley, Robert, 78
"Know-it-all" behavior, 149
Koen, Deb, 78

Leaders. *See also* Managers
  anger in, 34
  commitments made by, 135–136
  conflict resolution skills of, 75
  courage of, 41, 42
  empathy of, 59
  flexibility and adaptability of, 102–103, 104–105, 106–107
  followers of, 112
  goal orientation abilities of, 95
  influence on goal achievement, 121–125, 126
  influence on the work climate, 116–121, 126
  "know-it-all" behavior of, 149
  lack of courtesy, 17
  performance-management techniques of, 123–124
Leadership
  dysfunctional, effects of, 116
  as personal influence competency, 10, 13, 112–116, 177
Leadership IQ, 1
Learned helplessness, 101
Learned Optimism (Seligman), 98
Learning, 74–75
Life scripts, 130
Listening, respectful, 12, 54–56, 62
  assessment of, 55–56, 62, 167–170
  for conflict resolution, 75
"Lone wolf" behavior, 148

"Managerial Moment of Truth," (Bodaken and Fritz), 39
Managers
  conflict resolution skills of, 75
  courage of, 41, 42
  flexibility and adaptability of, 102–103, 104–105, 106–107

goal orientation abilities of, 95, 98
instinct-based decision making by, 152
rescuing behavior of, 61–62
Manipulation, 48–49, 138, 145
Mastery of purpose and vision, 9, 11, 14,
  129–140, 160
  competencies associated with, 14
    authenticity, 14, 135–140, 160, 180
    taking actions toward one's purpose,
      133–135, 139, 160, 180
    understanding one's purpose and values,
      130–132, 139, 160, 180
  as foundation for emotional intelligence,
    130
  as internal function, 11
Michigan State University, 4
Morale, 36, 116, 117, 119

Narcissism, 90–91
Nestlé, 74

Observation skills, 19
Optimism, as personal influence competency,
  14, 86, 159
  assessment of, 98–101, 108, 175
  examples of, 99
Organizational savvy, as social expertness
    competency, 13–14, 66, 78–81
  assessment of, 79–81, 83, 171–174
  examples of, 78–79, 80–81
  role in career success, 78
Organizations, lack of direction of, 95

Past behavior, reflection on, 21–26
Peers, personal influence over, 125
Performance-management techniques,
  123–124
Personal influence, 8, 13–14, 86,159
  as basis for leadership, 10
  as external function, 10
  as influence on others, 111–127, 159
    creating a positive work climate compe-
      tency, 116–121, 126, 159, 177–180
    getting results through others
      competency, 121–125, 126–127, 159
    leadership competency, 112–116, 126,
      159
  as influence on self, 85–109, 159
    flexibility and adaptability competency,
      14, 86, 101–107, 108, 159, 175–178
    goal orientation competency, 86, 94–98,
      108, 159, 174
    initiative and accountability
      competency, 86, 91–94, 107, 159,
      173–176

optimism competency, 14, 86, 98–101,
  108, 159, 175
self-confidence competency in, 86–91,
  107, 159, 172–175
Personality, charming, 145
Physician-patient interactions, 17
Polman, Paul, 74
Power figures, over reliance on, 148
Promises, honoring of, 135
Purpose. *See* Mastery of purpose and vision

Quality movement, 55
Questions and answers, in emotional
    intelligence interviews
  for empathy assessment, 55–58, 60–62,
    167–171
  identification of trends in, 142–151
  for mastery of purpose and vision assess-
    ment, 130, 131–132, 133–135, 179–182
  for personal influence assessment, 159,
    172–176, 175–178, 177–181
    flexibility and adaptability, 103–107
    goal achievement/goal orientation,
      96–98, 122–125, 174
    initiative and accountability, 92–94,
      173–176
    leadership, 113–116, 177
    optimism, 99–101, 175
    positive work climate, 118–121, 177–180
  for self-awareness assessment
    emotional and inner awareness, 22–23,
      24, 162–165
    impact on others, 18–20, 168–171
    reflection on past behavior, 23–24, 25–26
    triggers to emotional reactions, 21, 23,
      24–25, 26
  for self-confidence assessment, 88–91,
    172–175
  for self-control assessment
    courage/assertiveness, 165–168
    emotional expression, 36–39, 164–167
    "in the moment" awareness, 45–47, 167
    planning the tone of conversations,
      47–49, 167
    resilience, 44–45, 166
  for social expertness assessment
    collaboration, 72–74, 170
    conflict resolution, 76–78, 82, 171
    courage/assertiveness, 40–42, 158–161
    organizational savvy, 79–81, 171–174
    relationship skills, 69–70, 82, 169–172

Recruiting firms, 142
Reflection, about past experiences, 23–24,
  25–26

Relationships
  building and sustaining of, 12, 66, 67,
    68–71, 74, 82
  flexibility in, 102
  management of, 129–130
  role in organizational savvy, 80
Rescuing behavior, 61–62
Resentment, as self-defeating emotion, 21
Resilience, as self-management competency,
    12, 42–45
  assessment of, 42–45, 50, 166
Resistance, 120, 124–125
Resumes, fraudulent or misleading, 141–142
Retention, of employees, 2, 116, 119

Sarcasm, 150
Self-awareness, 8, 11–12, 15–31, 157
  in combination with self-control, 36
  competencies associated with, 11, 16–24
    accurate self-assessment, 11, 16, 26–28,
      29–30, 157, 163–166
    emotional and inner awareness, 11, 16,
      20–26, 29, 157, 162–165
    impact on others, 11, 16–20, 29, 157,
      161–164
  effect on sales performance, 16–17
  interaction with self-control, 9
  as internal function, 9
  "in the moment," 45–47
  lack of, 16–18
Self-confidence
  lack of, 147–148
  as personal influence competency, 13,
    86–91, 107
    assessment of, 87–91, 107
    differentiated from arrogance, 87, 90
    examples of, 87–88
    relationship to narcissism, 90–91
Self-control, 8, 9, 11–12, 33–51
  in combination with self-awareness, 36
  competencies associated with, 12
    courage or assertiveness, 34, 39–42, 158,
      165–168
    emotional expression, 34, 35–39,
      157–160, 164–167
    "in the moment," 45–47, 167
    planning the tone of conversations, 34,
      47–49, 167
    resilience, 34, 42–45, 158, 166
  interaction with self-awareness, 9
Self-doubt, 147–148
Self-esteem, 2
Self-management. *See* Self-control

Self-talk, 21
Seligman, Martin, 146
Senge, Peter, 75
Service orientation, 12, 54, 58–62, 63, 94
  assessment of, 60–63, 169
Setting the Table (Meyer), 59
Skepticism, 150–151
Skills and abilities, self-awareness of, 11, 16
  assessment of, 27–30
Skills audits, 2
Social bonds, 10
Social expertness, 8, 12–13, 65–84, 158
  competencies associated with, 10, 12–13,
    66–84
    building relationships, 66, 68–71, 82,
      158, 169–172
    collaboration, 10, 12–13, 66, 71–74, 82,
      158, 170
    conflict resolution, 66, 74–78, 82, 158,
      171
    organizational savvy, 66, 67, 78–81, 83,
      158, 171–174
  as external function, 10
Social Intelligence (Albrecht), 68
Stress, job-related, 116

Teammates, 59, 75
Teamwork, aversion to, 148
Technical excellence/skills, 2–3, 78
Thoughts, relationship to behavior, 5
Trust, 135, 138

University of Texas, 152
University of Toledo, 151–152

Values, 139. *See also* Mastery of purpose and
    vision
  conflicted, 136, 138
  corporate/organizational, 34, 136
  one's understanding of, 130–132, 139
Verification, of job applicants credentials,
    141–142, 145–146
Victimization, feelings of, 146
Vision. *See* Mastery of purpose and vision

Work climate, positive, 13, 116–121, 126
  assessment of, 118–121, 126, 177–180
  benefits of, 116
  effect on job stress, 116
  examples of, 117
Workforce, older adults in, 1–2
World's Most Powerful Leadership Principles, The
    (Hunter), 115–116

ABOUT THE AUTHOR

Adele B. Lynn is the founder of The Adele Lynn Leadership Group, an international consulting and training firm that helps leaders forge trusting relationships. She is a frequent keynote speaker who inspires leaders to create an emotional climate conducive to high performance. Her company also provides resources for trainers, coaches, and human resource professionals. Her previous books include *The Emotional Intelligence Activity Book, The EQ Difference,* and *Quick EQ Activities for Busy Managers.* She lives in Belle Vernon, Pennsylvania.

For more information contact:
The Adele Lynn Leadership Group
609 Broad Ave.
Belle Vernon, PA 15012
724 929-5352
www.lynnleadership.com

Recommended SHRM Resources

Staffing Management magazine

For the latest techniques and trends in recruiting and retaining employees, HR experts turn to *Staffing Management*—the essential resource on recruiting and staffing. Subscriptions are $35 per year United States and its territories; $55 per year Canada; $85 per year international (via airmail). Visit www.shrm.org/staffingmanagement/magazine/ to order.

The Practical HR Kit

Solving the Compensation Puzzle: Putting Together a Complete Pay and Performance System
  By Sharon K. Koss, SPHR, CCP

Proving the Value of HR: How and Why to Measure ROI
  By Jack J. Phillips, Ph.D., and Patricia Pulliam Phillips, Ph.D.

Legal, Effective References: How to Give and Get Them
  By Wendy Bliss, J.D., SPHR

Investigating Workplace Harassment: How to Be Fair, Thorough, and Legal
  By Amy Oppenheimer, J.D., and Craig Pratt, MWS, SPHR

The Source Book Kit

Employment Termination Source Book
  By Wendy Bliss, J.D., SPHR, and Gene Thornton, Esq., PHR

Performance Appraisal Source Book
  By Mike Deblieux

Hiring Source Book
  By Cathy Fyock, CAP, SPHR

Trainer's Diversity Source Book
  By Jonamay Lambert, M.A., and Selma Myers, M.A.

HIPAA Privacy Source Book
  By William S. Hubbartt, SPHR, CCP

TO ORDER SHRM BOOKS

SHRM offers a member discount on all books that it publishes or sells. Bulk purchase discounts are also available for SHRM-published books. To order these or any other book published by SHRM through the SHRMStore:

ONLINE: www.shrm.org/shrmstore

BY PHONE: 800-444-5006 (option #1); or
                  770-42-8633 (ext. 362); or
                  TDD: 703-548-6999